An Architectural Guidebook Great Malvern Worcestershire

Author

Louisa Davidson MA BA (Hons) ALCM AssocIHBC

1

Contents

List of Figures

Acknowledgements

The Worcester Archaeology and Archive Historic Environment Record Department particularly Emma Hancox and The Malvern Civic Society volunteers Brian Iles, Philip Duckworth, Malcolm Robinson, Philip Robinson, John Roslington and Bob Tilley who helped the author with the 'Buildings of Worcestershire Project' and survey of Malvern November 2013-June 2014 on behalf of HER Worcester. In particular, thanks to local historian and photographer Brian Iles. Thanks to the Malvern Library Local Archive. Thanks to Harriet Devlin MBE Head of the Historic Environment Conservation Masters Course Ironbridge 2012-14 for encouragement in undertaking the original Guide that this updated version is based on.

Author Louisa Davidson

Introduction

The buildings in Malvern chosen for this Architectural Guide all fall into the following style categories Medieval,C17,Georgian, Regency, Victorian, Edwardian and C20 and C21 and they still retain most of their character features and have a special architectural or historic interest. The survey for the Guide was compiled over a period of 9 months covering most of Malverns two Conservation Areas, Great Malvern and Trinity. This is a celebration of Malverns Architecture.

Great Malvern is a pattern book of 'typical' but varied architectural styles within a relatively small area. 'A real open air 'lived in' Building Museum'. This unique architectural living museum and its surroundings was so carefully laid out and stipulated by the Victorian Lady Foley, an early 'garden city pioneer of her day' (Hurle, 1985) (Smith, 1964)

The Architecture of Malvern

MR. A. TROYTE GRIFFITH'S LECTURE.

AT MEETING OF THE S.E.C.

" The best and most characteristic feature of Malvern is the general lay-out of the district on Garden City lines. Nowhere will you find 50 yards of closely built houses on both sides of a road. Malvern must have been at least fifty years ahead of any other town in England in avoiding the worst result of the 19th century commercialism—the creation of slum areas!"

This observation was made last week by Mr. A. Troyte Griffith, in the course of an address on " The Architecture of Malvern," at a meeting of the the Society for Education in Citizenship.

Fig 1 Troyte Griffith Local Architect Malvern Gazette Headline 1935
Source: Malvern Gazette cutting 1935

There are buildings that fall into the categories that have not been included either because they are similar to the ones chosen or there have been too many changes to distinct style features such as replacement UPVC windows and doors and modern extensions The HER Survey 'Buildings of Worcestershire Project' led by the author with volunteers from Malvern Civic Society was a resource for many buildings in the guide from the period up to 1885. Many others post dating this 1st Edition Ordnance Survey map were surveyed and described separately by the author and have been included in this Guide. Many are buildings from the Edwardian and Arts & Crafts period and the C20th and C21st Century.

Since completed the Survey for the Guide the author has qualified as an Historic Building Consultant having gained an MA in Historic Environment Conservation with distinction from the University of Birmingham. The author is currently practising as a freelance Historic Building Conservation Consultant.

Malvern began life as a village centred around the Benedictine Monastery and Priory and did not grow until the beginning of the C19 mainly due to the towns wealth and prosperity as a Spa town, chiefly in the 19th century, and the towns unique positioning within an area of outstanding natural beauty, the Malvern Hills. The town saw in the past wealthy individuals spend lavishly on villas of all styles, shapes and sizes with no expense spared. The Classical and Gothick Regency buildings are mostly located around The Priory and along the Worcester Road and the majority were GDII listed in the 1970s. Due to the purity of the now famous 'Malvern Water and Springs' Malvern did not grow into a town until late C18 when 'Malvern' was put on the map, consequently most early villas date from the Regency period and are listed. Most other buildings are unlisted. Most fall within the towns Conservation Areas and date from the later Victorian/Edwardian periods. An increase in building in C19 happened with the coming of the 'water cure doctors' and hydropathy (Nott, 1900)which continued through to the Arts and Crafts period up to 1910 even when the water cure/spa town businesses dwindled.   This building spread out downhill East below the Regency area. No Street is the same; most are individually designed Villas, a mix of Classical Victorian, Gothic, High Gothic and late Victorian / c1900-14 Arts & Crafts, a real battle of the styles. There are very few terraced properties due to Lady Foleys covenants. '*Lady Emily Foley- the Lord of the Manor-severely controlled the kind of houses built within a mile of the Priory. So, was she not one of Englands first town planners?*' (Rt Hon The Earl Beauchamp, 1953) Many private schools set up in the early 20th century were often housed in the previous 'hydropathy' lodgings that sprang up during the height of the 'water cure'. (Hurle, 1985) People either settled in the town in the already large Villas or had new ones built some by well-known architects such as Voysey and local architect Troyte Griffith. (Pevsner, Alan Brooks and Nicolas, 2007) Malvern was regenerated again in the 1920s and 30s by George Bernard Shaw and Elgar with an annual Festival (Smith, 1964)and there are a few architectural examples from this period. After World War II Malvern had some post war social housing built 'Homes for Heroes' and there are small estates still surviving, although some 'Cornish' housing units are to be demolished. Malvern has a few notable 1960s and 70s buildings. There has been some inevitable infill of later C20 and C21 buildings. Some are worthy of note and have also been included in this Architectural Guide.

All photographs unless stated are the authors and all were taken specifically for this Guide and from the public highway.

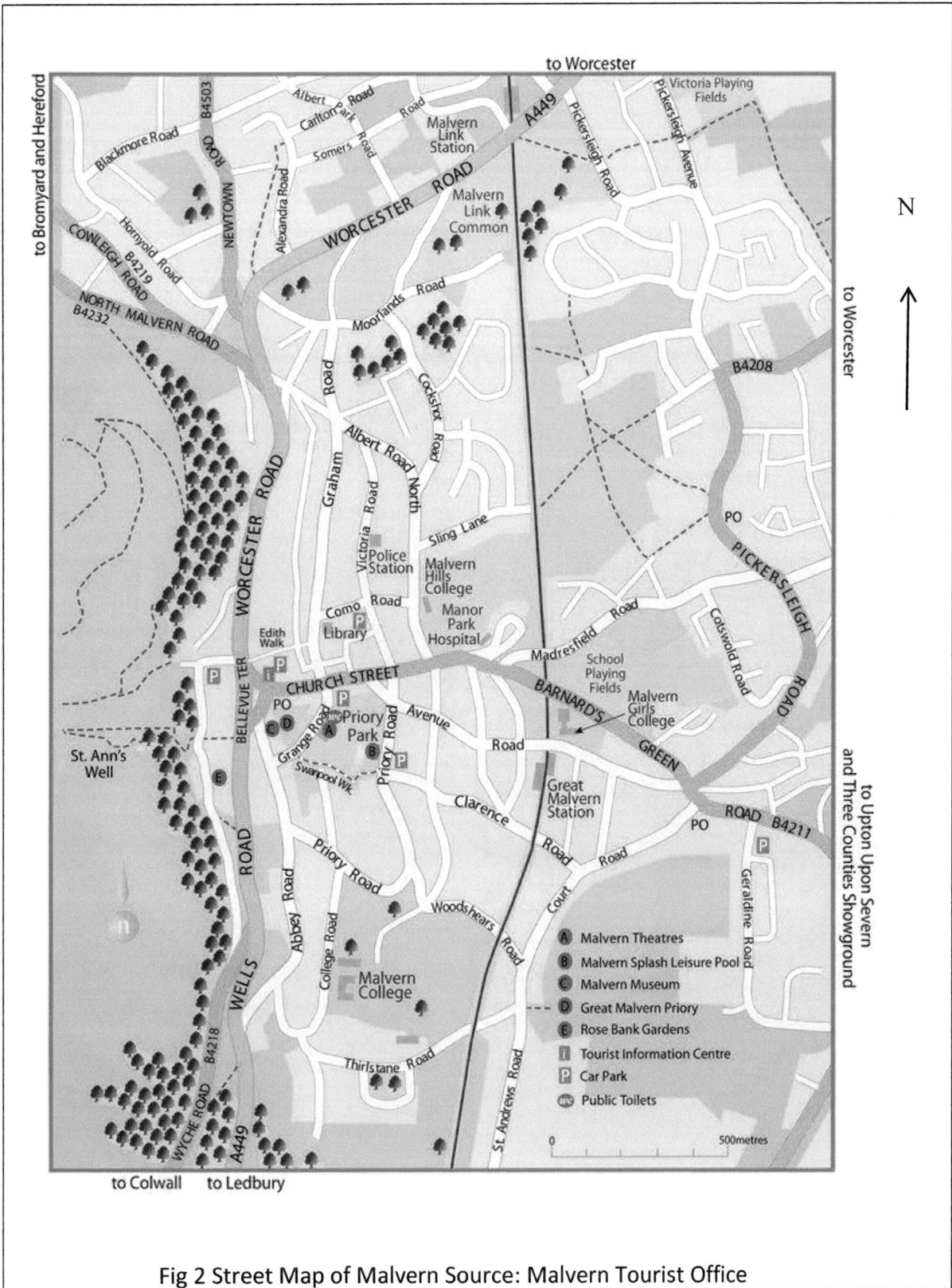

Fig 2 Street Map of Malvern Source: Malvern Tourist Office

Fig 3 Medieval Style Parts & C17
Using Buildings from Malvern Source: Author

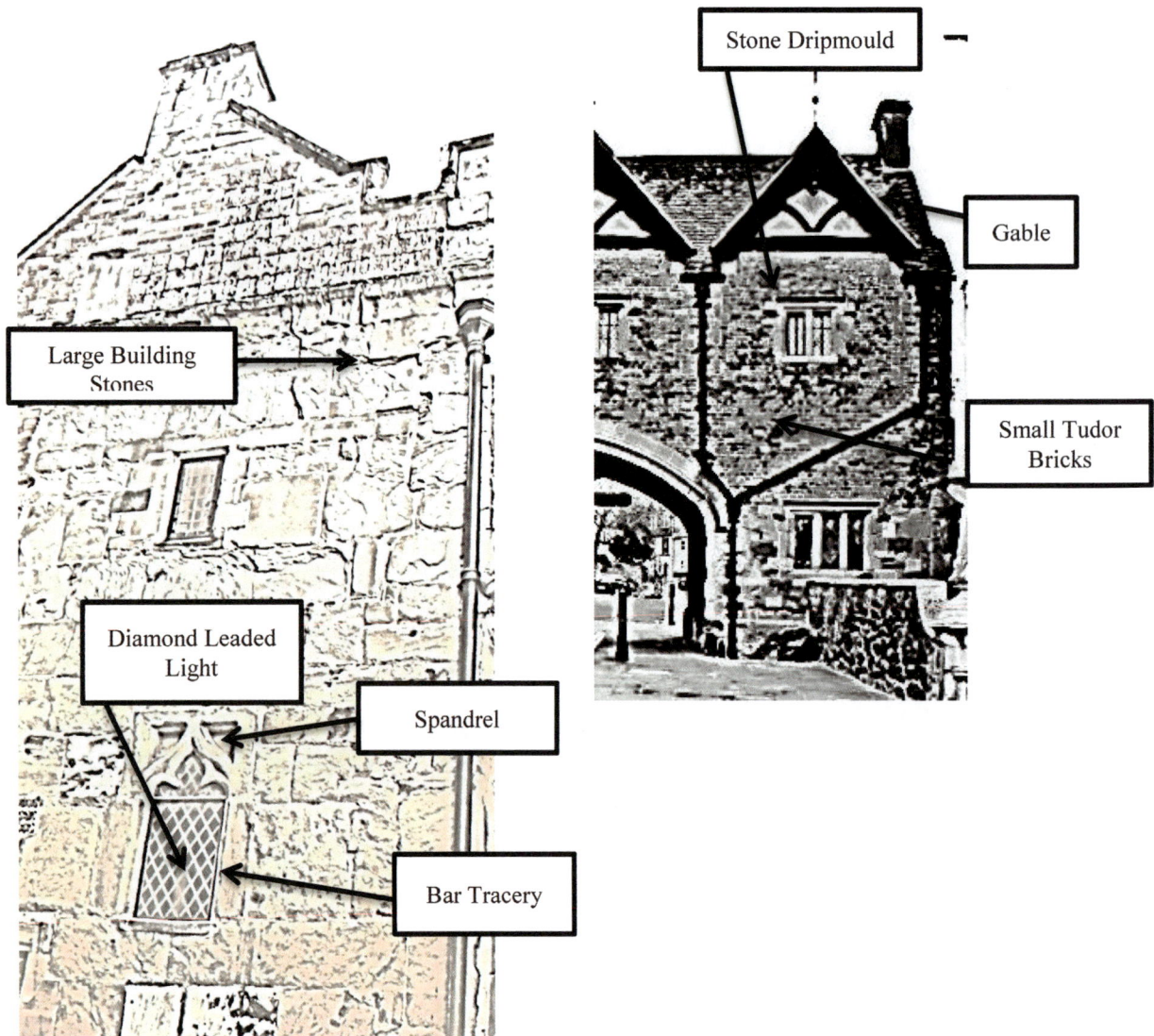

Stone Dripmould

Gable

Small Tudor Bricks

Large Building Stones

Diamond Leaded Light

Spandrel

Bar Tracery

In Medieval times Great Malvern consisted probably of a few crofts or cottages and a little Church date of construction unknown. (Smith, 1964) The site was remote when establishing the Monastery in 1276. The first map by Worcester map maker Joseph Doherty marked the Abbey Gateway in 1725 and his brother John marked it on a map in 1744. Although the Abbey Gateway/Priory Gatehouse was refaced in the C19 it along with some parts of the Priory are all that remain physically from this mediaeval time

MANORS

'The manor of GREAT MALVERN is not entered in the Domesday Survey. A monastery is said to have been founded here in the reign of Edward the Confessor. The site of the priory was confirmed to the monks by Edward the Confessor, William I and Henry I, the latter in 1127–8 granting quittance for assarts made in the forest with land in Baldenhall. His charter was confirmed by Edward II in 1320–1 and by Edward III in 1376 In 1276 the prior was returned as owner of Great Malvern, the extent of which was estimated in 1291 at 4 carucates of land. At the dissolution of the priory the clear annual value of the manor of Great Malvern was £67 9s. 8½d. It was held by the Crown till 1547, when it was leased for twenty-one years by Edward VI to Thomas Fisher. In 1554 Queen Mary granted the manor in reversion to John Lord Lumley, and this grant was confirmed by Queen Elizabeth in 1585. In the same year Lord Lumley had licence to alienate it to Henry Bromley of Holt, and the sale was effected in 1586. For many years after the Dissolution Malvern was a small and unimportant village. In 1562–3 it contained 105 families, while Newland had 13. By the 17th century the Malvern waters were beginning to be known for their curative propertie ' (http://www.british-history.ac.uk/report.aspx?compid=42867#n28, 2014)

A time of great Cathedral building, for example at Salisbury, Canterbury, Wells and Lincoln and the building of Abbey Churches in an Early Gothic Style. The impact of northern France on English medieval architecture saw the beginnings of the Decorated and Perpendicular style late in the C13 when earlier Cathedrals were added to with decorated cloisters rather than functional ones. (Watkin, 1979) Great skill was needed by the stone masons. The Vernacular style was far humbler, for example medieval timber framed thatched open halls often with two bays for the more wealthy usually of cruck construction. This construction was also used in cottages and barns, the most prestigious surviving today. The carpenters were equally skilled in constructing timber frames in this period. (Harris, 1978) (Brunskill, n.d.)

1.3 The Tudor House Style

1485-1560 saw a great change in style and the creation of the Church of England after the dissolution of the Monasteries. Villages were dominated by the Manor House/two storey farmhouses (hall with cross wings or box framing) whilst for the majority the style was simple buildings of timber, mud or rubble stone. For some, buildings were of the finest timber framing featuring close vertical studding becoming more and more decorated to demonstrate wealth. Urban houses often displayed a jetty to gain extra room on upper floors. Introduction of bricks, typically red, often dressed with stone surrounds for windows.

1.4 The Elizabethan Style

1560-1660. Masonry and brick were used more prolifically for large manor houses and farm houses but the majority still lived in simpler often one storey timber framed cottages but now with added external chimney stacks. Larger mullion and transom windows with leaded lights for the wealthier population, simple casements for most but often too with leaded lights/glass.

By the end of the century [1660-1714] sometimes referred to as the Restoration Period there was a move towards Classical symmetrical architecture and a 'Dutch style' , red bricks, stone quoins, stone facades and pediments above windows and doors, early sash windows with 9, 12 or 16 lights set in a wooden box. Only the lower sash moved. This classical style of building in the late C17 being a pre cursor for the popular Georgian style of Architecture.

1.5 Materials

The Cathedrals, Monasteries and early churches used local stone (sandstone or limestone). For timber framed buildings oak was preferred but other timber was also used such as Elm. By the Tudor and Elizabethan period there was more use of bricks and stone, oak still being used for window frames and doors and internal walls and floors

1.6 Materials used in Malvern in relation to style.

There is not a lot of surviving early material left in the Priory or Gatehouse but the earliest stone is said to be green and red sandstone. The Gatehouse has some Tudor brick work. Brick and tile making is recorded in 1610 by Richard Haynes of Great Malvern (Smith, 1964) As Malvern was only a small village until the Regency period buildings pre dating this have rarely survived. However a few timber framed cottages/inns of the C17 have been found and have been included in the appraisal section of this Guide.

1.7 Malvern Architects

1460 Priory Church rebuilt by Sir Reginald Bray architect to Henry V11 Westminster Abbey Chapel

That munificent patron of the fine arts, Sir Reginald Bray, K. G. a native of Worcester was the architect; and under his superintendence the church assumed that appearance and character which still render it the admiration of beholders, who, from its magnificent remains, may conceive an idea of its pristine beauty. (Southall, 1825)

1460 Abbey Gateway, northern part of the Gateway built by stone Masons after re building the church porch *'skilfully designed to harmonise with the great church'* (Griffith, 1940)

Vernacular and later buildings – Architects unknown

Note The Gatehouse a GD II* Listed building and Scheduled Monument was refaced in the C19 but earlier stones remain under the Arch.

Fig 4 Malvern Gatehouse Photos: Author

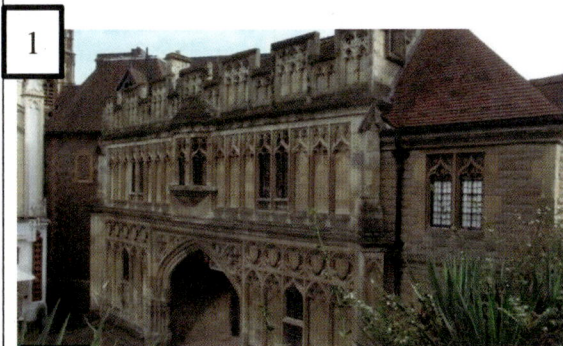

1145 Gateway First record of early timber framed Gatehouse building, Porter mentioned who occupied the upper storey and received visitors: Robert The Janitor and his successor John The Janitor in 1284 (Nott, 1885) Todays North elevation of the gateway is of 1860[1] filling space between dormers with thicker bricks and a new arch

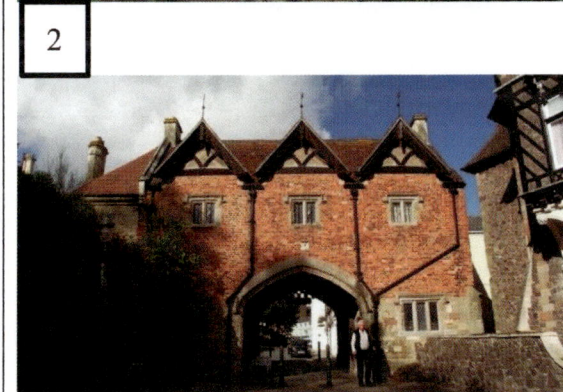

1545 William Pinnock under royal licence sold monastic buildings to John Knotsford a wealthy local landowner who demolished all but the Gatehouse and Guesten Hall. (Smith, 1964) Bequeathed to Daughter who married into the Savage family and became part of Savage Estate for 200 years.

C16 the arch [2] with original jambs and restored head and a drip mould has above its apex a small stone carving of an angel the same as on Knotsford tomb in the Priory. The stone mullioned Tudor windows [2] with drip moulds and splay moulding have square headed, 2-light diamond lattice iron casements. Stone on the ground floor and Tudor brickwork on the first floor in mostly English bond. Three Gables with decorative oak barge boards with iron finials.

1545-50 Gateway
Tudor reconstruction of Gatehouse.
Extended 2 m South side of gate posts with stone from other monastic buildings same as used on The Priory at the same time. Upper storey rebuilt with thin red bricks, ground floor sand stone, stone mullion windows on ground and upper storey .[2]

By 1871 the Gateway appears to have fallen into disrepair *'State of poor repair north stone falling into road The North side had got into a ruinous condition in about 1890 and was then refaced and addition made at the west end.'* (Griffith, 1935) (Stanley, 1852) [3] High up on this gable there are 64 mediaeval encaustic tiles below a string course or remains of original medieval stone parapet. Original C15 ogee medieval window.[3] This print [4] by Henry Lamb, Source: Malvern Library, shows the south side with the timber framed Gueston Hall to the east.

The Priory Church now GD II* Listed was consecrated in **1460** Bishop Carpenter of Worcester (Griffith, 1940)

In **1541 the** Priory church was bought by the people/ parishioners of Great Malvern for £20. Partial demolition of church was saved from destruction by parishioners '*the church and Belfry Chancel with aisles and chapels within the same church £20 paid in instalments* (Smith, 1964) By 1860 The Priory went under extensive restoration and repair by George Gilbert Scott.

Fig 5 Great Malvern Priory Church 2014 Source: Author

Fig 6 Sparrow 1787 Print Source: Malvern Library Collection

As for the Village of Malvern and the buildings of this period only very few remain. The Unicorn Inn GD II listed back in 1949 is said to be C16 timber-frame, with later additions '*painted brick, rendered to front elevation. Slate roof, two storeys.*' The C16 building is clearer on the rear west elevation and internally.

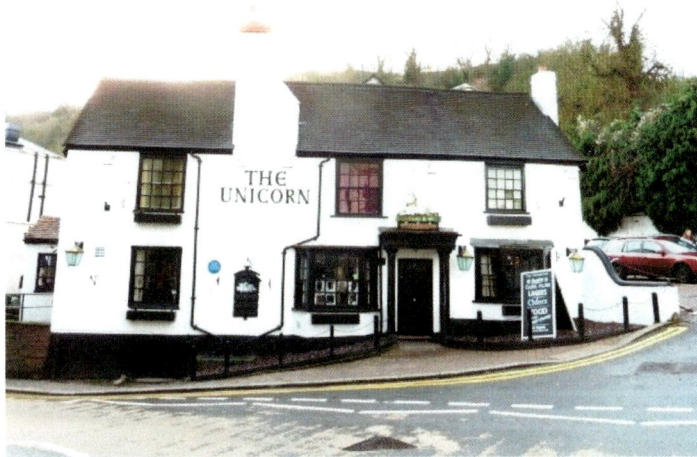

Fig 7 The Unicorn GDII Listed Public House
Source: Author

Fig 8 Lapwood Cottage GDII listed Source: Author

Fig 9 Lapwood above sometime in the 1920s. One of only two cottages remaining in the road. The building next door having disappeared Source: Malvern Library Collection

Pickersleigh Court GD II Listed dates from the C15. It was once a key Parliamentarian centre during the Civil War, when the house was in the middle of what was Malvern Chase. Pickersleigh Court, as mentioned in Pevsner Guides, is an extensive residence primarily of 15th century origins with 19th century additions.

It has historic associations to the Foley and Beauchamp Estates. North End Farm sprawled uncertainly from Spring Lane to Pound Bank and Pickersleigh had isolated fields (Smith, 1964)

Fig 10 Pickersleigh Court Source: Author

Fig 11 Pickersleigh House Source: Postcard

Barnards Green House

"The original Barnard's Green was to the east of what we now call Barnard's Green.
Doherty in 1744 wrote 'Barnets Green' at the spot where the roads from Malvern, Poolbrook and Guarlford converge by the pond since named Hastings Pool" (Hurle, 1985)

Fig 12 Barnards Green House Source: Author

Parts of Barnards Green House ,GD II Listed, date back to 1630. It was formerly known as Balders Hall, Balders Green and appears on 1744 Doherty Map. Occupied by the Dandridge Family and leased from Foley Estates in the C18. Hastings Pool to the East of the house was later named after Charles Hastings who retired to this house in the 1860s and died there in 1866. Charles Hastings was founder of the British Medical Association. (Hurle,1985) (Smith, 1964)

Architectural Description:

'Mid C18 stucco front to earlier fabric. Two storeys, tile roof, moulded eaves cornice. Rusticated quoins. Three arched casement windows. Stuccoed Tuscan porch with pediment, modillion cornice and chanelled frieze extended along inner face to contain side lights. Wing with hipped roof at rear with 3-lightcanted bay and recessed door below. Three gables dated 1635. Interior stated to have C17 panelling and overmantel'. (National Heritage List for England, 2015)

NB Barnards Green House is also mentioned in 'Buildings of England Worcestershire' by author Alan Brooks in the updated Pevsner Series (Alan Brooks, 2007)

The GDII Curtilage Potting Shed sits within the grounds of Barnards Green House and dates back to the Pleasure Grounds before being used as an Horticultural building when the gardens gained a Kitchen garden in the C19

Fig 13 Potting Shed Source: Author

Fig 14. Georgian /C18 House Parts
Buildings from Malvern Source: Author

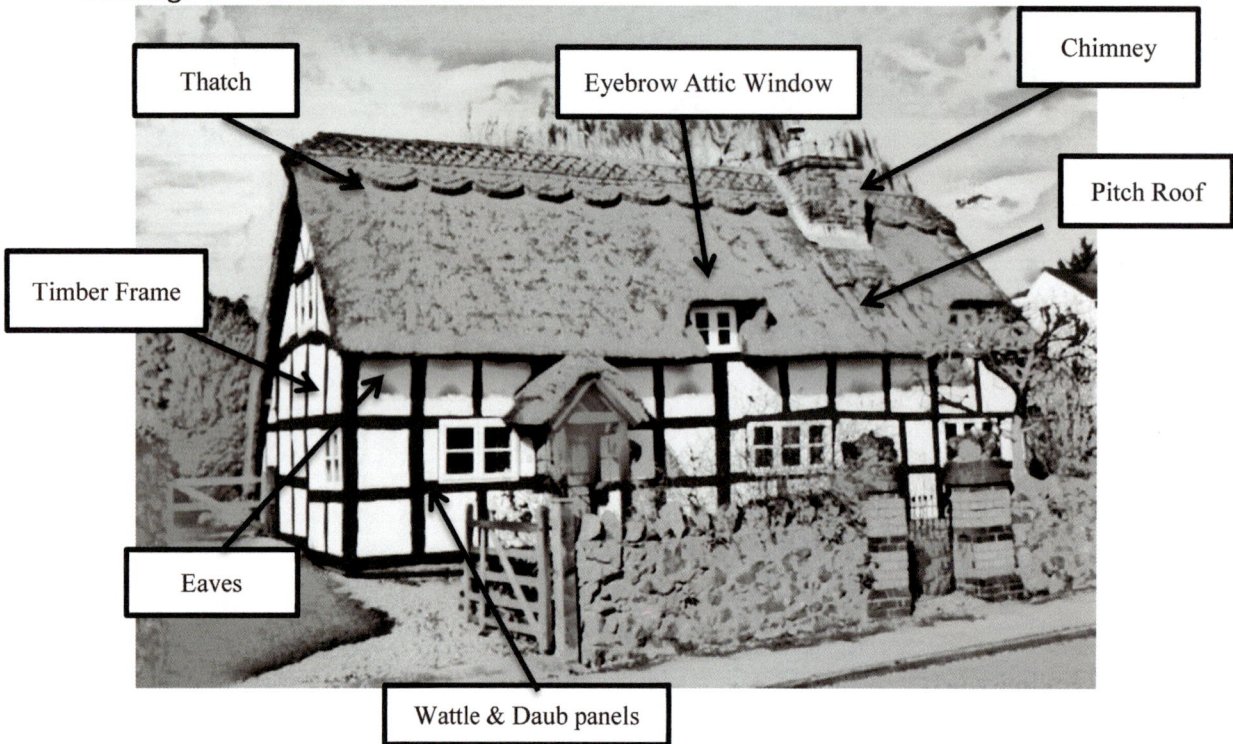

Thatch | Eyebrow Attic Window | Chimney | Pitch Roof | Timber Frame | Eaves | Wattle & Daub panels

Classical Style at Croome Court Near Malvern [owner National Trust]

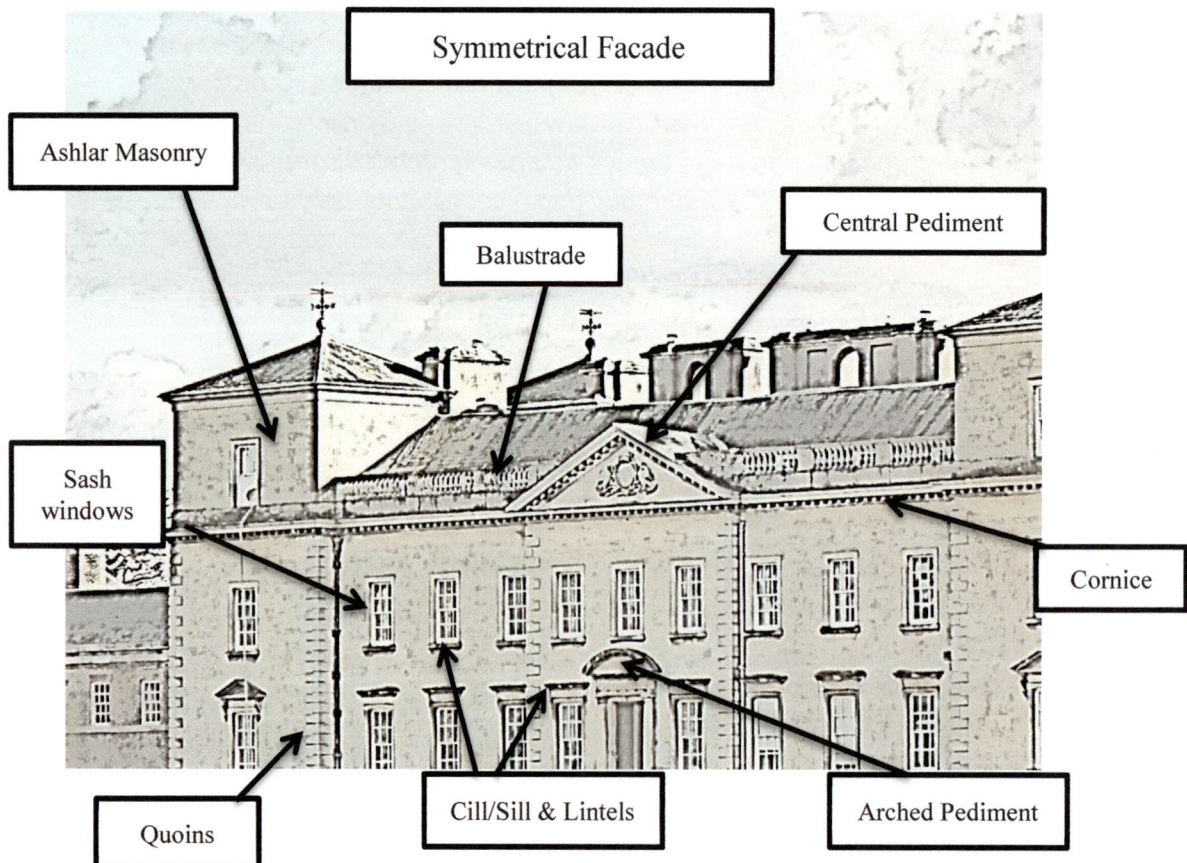

Symmetrical Facade | Ashlar Masonry | Balustrade | Central Pediment | Sash windows | Cornice | Quoins | Cill/Sill & Lintels | Arched Pediment

2. 1 Historical Note/Context

Land belonged in Malvern to The Lygons of Madresfield later bought by the Beauchamps in the C19. The Hornyolds at Blackmore and Hanley Castle and The Foleys in 1741, the first Lord Foley seat was a Stoke Edith in Herefordshire (Smith, 1964)

In 1776 there were 120 families, and in 1782 only 100. The village of Malvern gradually became a Spa and by 1801 there were 819 persons (Smith, 1964)

2.2 The Style

The Georgian style was typically tall Palladian (named after the C16 Architect Palladio) terraces in the towns and the growth of fashionable resorts for example at Bath. Elegant but plain facades, symmetrical and proportioned, rustication, columns, capitals, pediment doorways, semi-circular fanlights, sash windows recessed later behind brick by the Building Act 1774 to stop the spread of fire. (Early examples maybe still flush.) Bow windows used for shops. For C18 domestic vernacular the author R.W.Brunskill describes

'Four categories; the Great House, the Large House, the Small House and the Cottage'…. 'imposing country seats of the 18C …… Small houses…the ordinary yeoman or tenant farmer, the miller, the smith, the shopkeeper, the schoolteacher were people of significance in the village, they lived in Small Houses' (R.W.Brunskill, 1970)

2. 3 Materials

Cut and carved locally sourced stone, handmade fired bricks, sash windows typically 6/6, lunettes and Venetian windows. Rusticated lime renders to look like stone. Materials varied from town to country due to sourcing materials as this was not yet the age of the train.

2. 4 Vernacular Materials

Walling construction of timber framed wattle and daubed panels and stone of irregular type. Brick spread to areas formerly dominated by timber construction in spite of Brick Taxes from varying degrees from 1784 until 1850. Roofing materials- thatch was the universal material, a light material not needing massive roof construction. Slates- during the second half of the C18 with improved water transport, sought after as being inflammable in towns. Stone flags mostly of sandstone in origin on low pitched roofs and graduated in size. Stone tiles were laid steeper. Plain Tiles made from clay with the development of brick making and used when slate and stone were unavailable. Plan form was double pile by the middle of the C18 and had spread to all parts of the country and levels of society. Windows were casements and vertical sliding sash (R.W.Brunskill, 1970)

2. 5 Materials used in Malvern in relation to style.

Typical vernacular details from the West Midlands, half timbering with square panels, prominent chimney breasts projecting from the gable walls designed for thatch with tiny first floor windows tucked under a deep eaves (Brunskill, 1981) The River Severn was nearby in Upton and materials may have been bought on boats called Trows.

2.6 Malvern architects

Unknown particularly as Malvern was still a hamlet centred around the Priory.

Photos: Author

Georgian architecture did not really come to Malvern even though notable Architects built country mansions nearby such as Croome Court. However, many of the surviving vernacular older cottages in Malvern date from the C18. The GD II Listed Mount Pleasant Hotel with Orangery, a former Inn, has a typical Georgian façade .It is said to be late Georgian in origin.

Fig 15 Mount Pleasant Hotel Belle Vue Terrace

Mount Pleasant Orangery nearly was demolished but was saved by Malvern Civic Society Source: MCS Archives

Today 2014 it is privately owned

Here are some of the best earlier surviving timber framed cottages in the survey area similar to those mentioned by the author R.W.Brunskill, one still with a thatched roof. All are GDII listed. There are many more on the outskirts of town

Fig 16 C18 Cottage styles in Malvern

[1] Brompton Cottage in Bank Street typical box frame timber framed cottage with external chimney stack [2] Priors Cottage 60 Court Road GDII listed C18 two storey (3) Clumber Cottage also in Court Road GDII Listed

Fig 17.Regency House Parts

Buildings from Malvern Source: Author

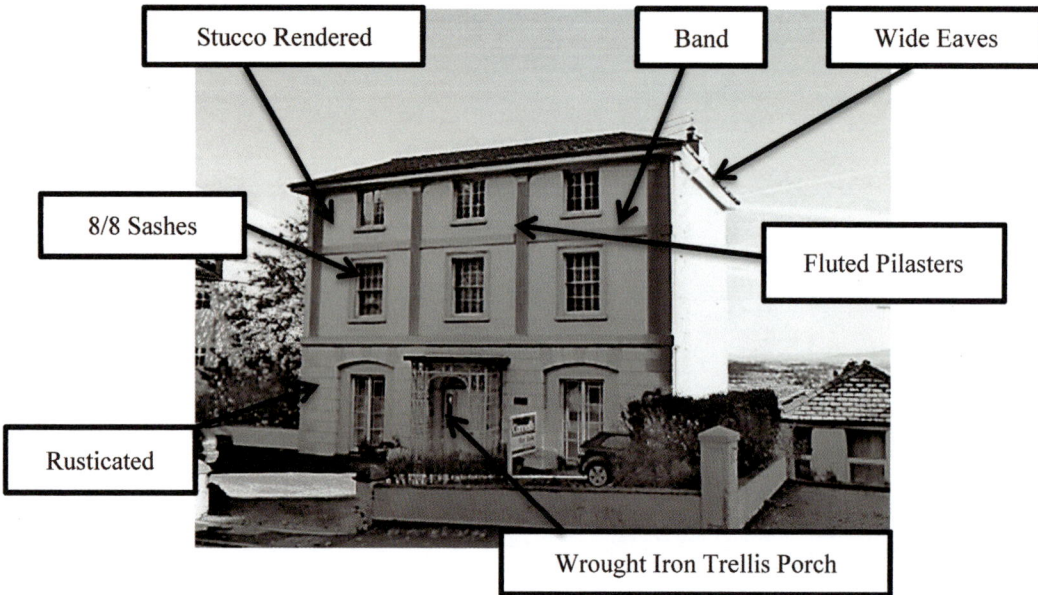

Stucco Rendered

Band

Wide Eaves

8/8 Sashes

Fluted Pilasters

Rusticated

Wrought Iron Trellis Porch

6/6 Sashes Not recessed

Semi-circular Bow Bay window with 3 moulded wood windows

3.1 Historical Note/Context

Great Malvern was inherited by Thomas Foleys second son Edward, who died in 1808. His son Edward Thomas Foley, who was lord of the manor in 1813, died in 1846.

The first guidebook for visitors appeared in 1796 while the centre was at Holy Well for the purity of the water for drinking. In 1796 The Crown and Mount Pleasant on Belle Vue Terrace were open to visitors but the growth really begun in 1810. Samuel Deykes designed The Foley Hotel, The Pump Room and Baths and they were built 1815-1819, John Deykes designed the Library and Assembly Rooms (likely to be Samuel Deykes son). It was built in 1819-1823. The elegant houses along Worcester Road sprung up to accommodate the increasing number of visitors (Smith, 1964)

The author Mary Southall in 1825 gives us a glimpse into the village of Great Malvern during the Regency period. She describes the ancient Gateway, The Hills and Inns and Boarding Houses and was an instigator in promoting Malvern to the wider public, including describing walks on the hills and further 'rides' further afield.

To pass unnoticed the admirable situation in which the village stands would be unpardonable ;on one hand the towering majestic hills, almost hangs over it; and the interesting Church beneath, exhibits, in its architecture, a very beautiful example of the latest period of the pointed style...............

This charming village is found, both by the inhabitant and sojourner, a very pleasing residence, and, in the season, is generally filled with company who visit the place, either for its romantic beauties, salubrious air, or healing waters. The aspect of the place is so favourable to vegetation that you may commonly see in the front of the houses, the Chinese rose and hydrangea in full bloom at Christmas. (Southall, 1825)

'The young Princess Victoria stayed at Holy Mount in Malvern during the summer of 1830...Mother and daughter approved the naming of a path to The Worcestershire Beacon as Victoria Walk' (Hurle, 1985.54)

3.2 The Style

The Style was Neo Classicism taking inspiration from the classical orders, Doric, Ionic, (spiral scroll shape on the capital), Corinthian (acanthus leaves) columns, (often fluted) porticos (glorified porches), entablatures, modillions, pediments and balustrades, pilasters (when a column is a fake column and not structural and has a flat profile on an elevation.) Decorative Wrought iron balconies and verandas were vogue. Roofs often appear to be flat behind parapets as they became shallow pitched or hipped on semis and detached houses, elevations were lime stucco rendered, multi paned windows(some bowed) with fine glazing bars were fashionable, so too six panelled doors and decorative fanlights above. (Parissien, 1992) (Cole, 2003) (Loudon, 1833)A delight in the picturesque and rustic also gave rise to the Cottage Orne, an idealised country dwelling

Common were brick elevations covered in lime render ashlar stucco often with banded mouldings. Grander houses were built with dressed ashlar stone to elevations. Stone columns and pediments, pilasters, window sills and balustrades were common, wrought iron balconies and verandas. Sash windows with fine moulded glazing bars. (Parissien, 1992) (Watkin, 1979 revised 2001) (Yorke, 2008)

Fig 18 Regency Style Malvern Style Source: Malvern Library Directories

3.4 Materials used in Malvern in relation to style.

Mostly used was local brick covered in lime render ashlar stucco often with banded mouldings. Some use of Roman cement and Coade stone. Some dressed ashlar stone to elevations for some buildings. [For example, 'The Firs' on Wells Road.] The use of stone columns and pediments, window sills and balustrades, and parapets hiding roofs. Some wrought iron balconies and verandas for example at the rear of Trafalgar House, Worcester Road and at Holyrood House on Wells Road.

3.5 Malvern architects

Some of Malverns Classical Regency Architecture could have been by Architects from Cheltenham as they were actively designing there nearby; Malvern was seen as a rustic retreat from Cheltenham. Samuel Whitfield Daukes is one example. He was also later responsible for Witley Court.(1850)

Photos: Author unless stated

Fig 19 Rosebank House before it was demolished in 1958. A fine example of a now lost Regency Villa. Source: Malvern Gazette 1957

Fig 20 1914 Jardin Public , Malvern Angleterre. Rosebank House above the gardens
1914 Source: Malvern Library Archive Directories
It was gifted to the town by CW Dyson Perrins after the WW1

Most of the rest of Malverns Regency Architecture is statutory Listed at GDII. Here are a few of the best.

Fig 21 Regency Examples in Malvern Photos: Author

1

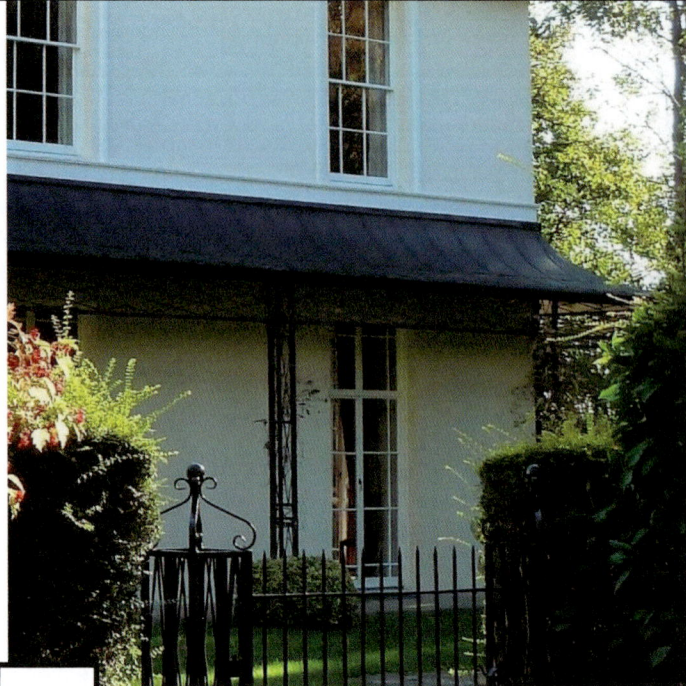

2

98 Stokefield, Graham Road [1&2]GDII Listed
Large 3 storey regency style villa divided into two. Slate hipped roof on brackets. Rendered elevations. Lead roofed veranda/canopy with cast iron details.6/6 pane sash windows to upper storey, French casement windows to lower storey

3

4

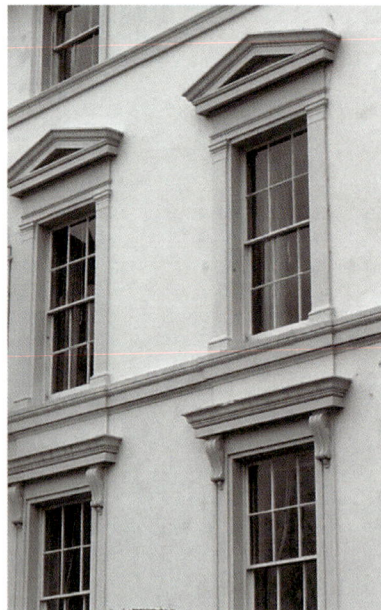

2 Bank Street GD II Listed Tent-canopied porch with wrought-iron trellis supports. (3) 23,Montrose Hotel Graham Road GD II pediment Five windows in moulded surrounds, hung sashes with glazing bars, in architraves with pilasters and pediments to 1st floor, (4)

Fig 22 Regency Examples on Worcester Road Malvern Photos: Author

54 Worcester Road (Aucott House GDII [1 & 2]Ground floor rusticated divided into 3 bays by fluted pilasters Central elliptical-headed doorway with fanlight,

Wrought-iron trellis porch.

Burford House Worcester Road GDII (3)
C1810
2,6,8 Worcester Road GDII
c1818   (4)
Architects Samuel and John Deykes. Originally the Royal Library. Three storeys in stucco with slate roofs. Elevation to south is bow-fronted; projecting semi-circular ground floor with balustraded entablature, frieze and moulded cornice, on 4 Ionic columns

Adapted for Barclays Bank 1930 Architect Guy Pemberton
(Alan Brooks, 2007)
Photos :Author

Bello Sequardo Foley Terrace GD II Listed.
Two full-height semi-circular bows with 3
moulded wood windows.
*Stuccoed Villa of 1833 altered by J.H.Strudwick
& Son 1893* (Alan Brooks, 2007)

37 Priory Road GD II Listed Early c19 Villa c1818,[3] Slate hipped roof, stucco render with
projecting central gable with pediment. Original 6/6 sash windows including rare x2 full
height bow window bays to ground level and fine fanlight over entrance door.

Fig 24 Unlisted Regency of Note Photos: Author

1

Melton Lodge 29Wells Road c1818 [1] To the rear 4 storey Bow Bays.

2

The Firs Wells Road 1825

Originally a very large Regency lodging house for visitors in the Spa days.
The house is 1825 Ashlar façade 2+3+2 bays the centre projecting beneath a shallow pediment with infilled porch with attached Ionic columns; moulded architraves and cornice, rusticated ground floor. Enlarged by J.A. Chatwin c1890-5 (Alan Brooks, 2007)

Fig 25 Regency Gothick House Parts
Buildings from Malvern Source: Author

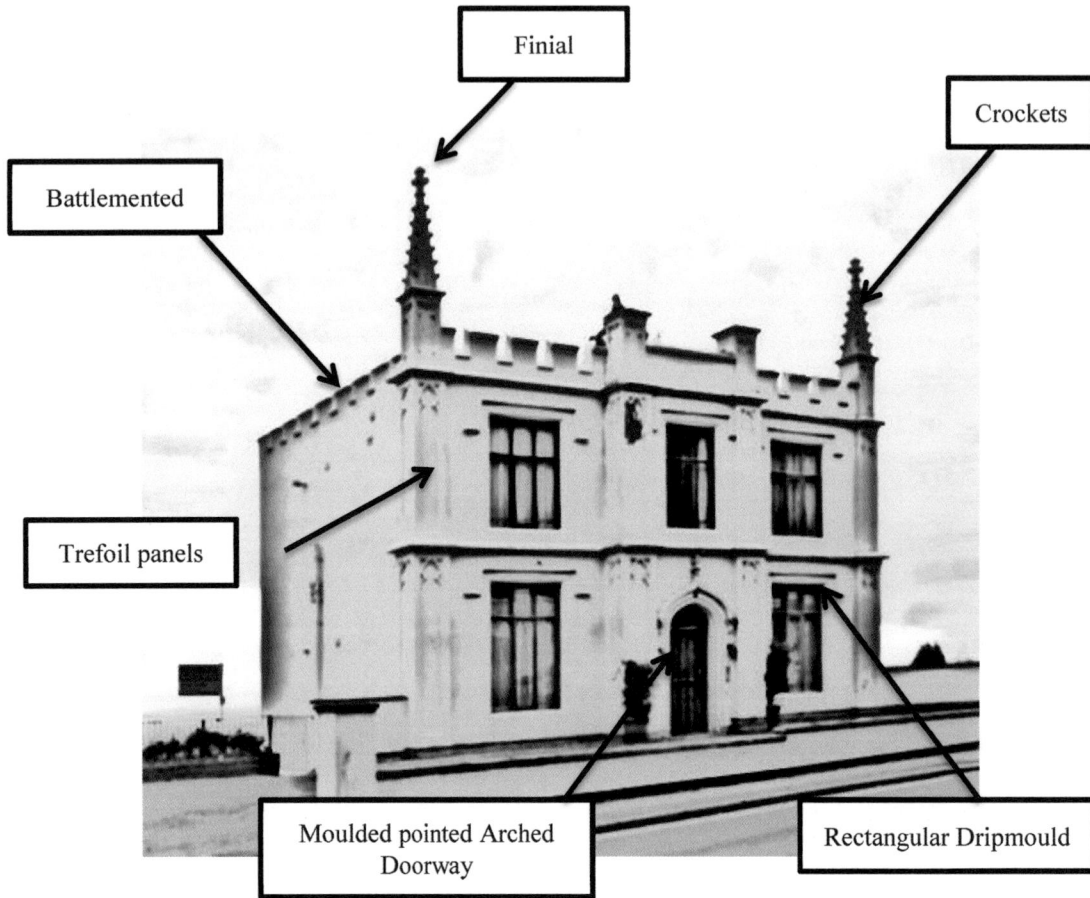

Finial

Crockets

Battlemented

Trefoil panels

Moulded pointed Arched Doorway

Rectangular Dripmould

During the 18th century people came to Malvern for the purity of its water.

'They found the Priory in a most dilapidated state. Through a veil of ivy,moss,fungus, and rubble fallen from the ceiling, they must have discovered, with joy of explorers, that the hidden and decaying building was a magnificent structure. Gothic architecture was just beginning to be appreciated again for the first time since the Renaissance.......influenced by this, Malvern builders from this time pledged their allegiance to the Gothic Revival for the domestic buildings which were by then appearing in the village spa' (Moody, 1953.13) (Moody, 1953)

This Gothick movement included variety : the villa, italianate style,castellated style, the pictureque in the town, as found in Malvern and the sham castle- a vision/ fantasy. (Eastnor Castle, Ledbury.) It was not a surprising that 'gothick' style was built in Malvern especially around the Priory and Gatehouse. Here we see Crockets, finials, battlements, trefoils in stone, rectangular and arched dripmoulds around windows and doors

4.2 Materials

Stone, lime rendered stucco and sometimes roman cement. Limewashed exterior elevations.

4.3 Materials used in Malvern in relation to style.

Mostly local brick covered in lime render stucco and roman cement used for dripmoulds, rectangular and arched.

4.4 Malvern Architects

Responsible for much of the building of this time in both Classical and Gothick was London Architect John Deykes. Mary Southall in 1825 describing the recently erected Library said *'The building adds very much to the respectability of Great Malvern, and has proved perfectly satisfactory to the proprietor, Mr. Foley, whose munificence first brought into professional notice, in this part of the country, Mr. John Deykes ,of London, the architect, to whom Great Malvern owes, whatever of grandeur or ornament the building has contributed'* (Southall, 1825) It is also possible that Architects and Builders came from Cheltenham, the centre for Regency Architecture in the early 19th century and not that far from Malvern and whose residents often made the trip to Malvern and The Hills.

Fortunately most of Malverns 'Gothick' buildings are listed although there are some plainer Tudor style villas that missed the mass listing in the 1970s. Of this 'Gothick' style in Malvern are, GD II listed 'Oriel Villa' on Worcester Road and 'Cridlin & Walker' once a butchers shop by the Priory Gateway [3], and 'Spa Villa' Priory Road 4] All feature battlements, stucco rendering and some crockets and finials.

Fig 26 .Gothick Examples in Malvern Photos: Author

The Old Butchers Shop with trefoiled panels and pinnacles with crockets and finials.

"Irregular stuccoed Gothic, with big canted bay, with pointed windows ,battlements and octagonal turret behind; later additions."
Brooks & Pevsner. (Alan Brooks, 2007)

The Tudor Gothick style was in keeping with the pattern books by JC Loudon 'Encyclopaedia of Villa Architecture' (Loudon, 1833) In 1833 came the later plainer 'gothick' villas , leaning more towards a revival 'Tudor' style but nevertheless still with 'gothick' overtones. Grange House in Priory Park and Holyrood House, Wells Road are typical examples.

The Grange,E side, behind a car park, irregular Tudor of c1830, has flat topped gables, an oriel, grouped brick chimneys, and,to the garden, a big square bay with semicircular projection. (Pevsner, Alan Brooks and Nicolas, 2007)

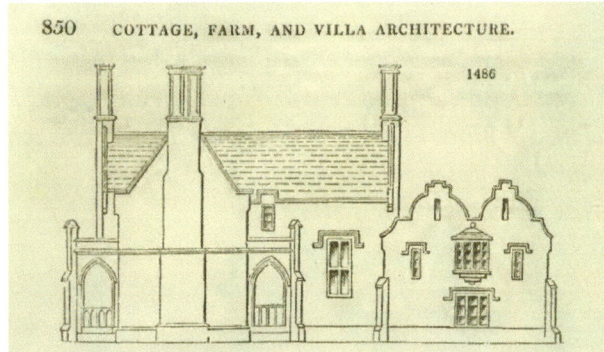

Fig 27 Gothic 1833 window
Source :JC Loudon[pg934 &850]Regency Gothic Villa JC Loudon

Fig 28 Examples of Tudor Gothick Style in Malvern 1-5 Photos: Author
(See how similar the buildings are to JC Loudons illustrations Fig 27 Above)

(1 & 2) Grange House Priory Park GDII listed
Circa 1830; in "Tudor' style. Two storeys and attics, rendered, with old tile roof.

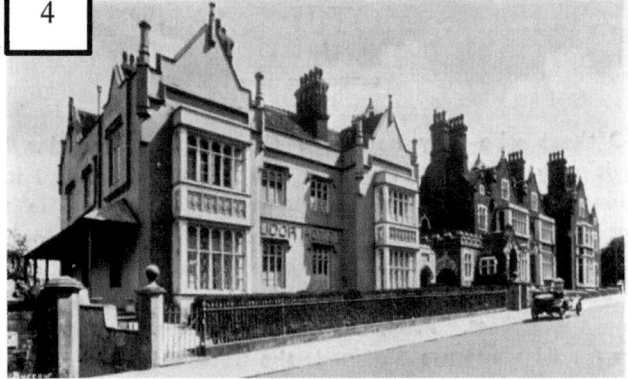

[3 & 4] 1,2 Holyrood House Wells Road GDII Listed (Photo[4] 1930s) Source: B.Iles Collection
Consists of 2 houses formerly known as Newbie House and Holyrood
House, joined by a bridge. Formerly the water cure establishment of Dr Gully,
who bought Newbie House for men and built Holyrood House for women and joined
them by a 'Bridge of Sighs', circa 1842 EH

(5) GD II Listed 1& 3 North Malvern Road in a Cottage Orne Gothick/Swiss Style.
Malvern is fortunate to have a few rarer examples of thatched Swiss style Lodges in Gothick
style c1820-30 as seen 1& 3 North Malvern Road and the unlisted 57 Wells Road Fig 29[3]

Fig 29 Regency Gothick Unlisted of Note 1-4

This is a large four storey gabled Tudor 'Gothick' with a 'k' style detached villa including garret storey [1] at 8, Abbey Road.
Number 10 Orchard Grange, Orchard Road [2] is another fine example. [3] 57 Wells Road ,unlisted, is very similar to the pretty 'Gothick Orne Swiss style' with thatched roof typical of Regency period like the example painted by Ackerman in his 'Gardens and Landscapes' Ackerman in 1820.[4]

Fig 30. Classical Victorian House Parts
Buildings from Malvern Source: Author

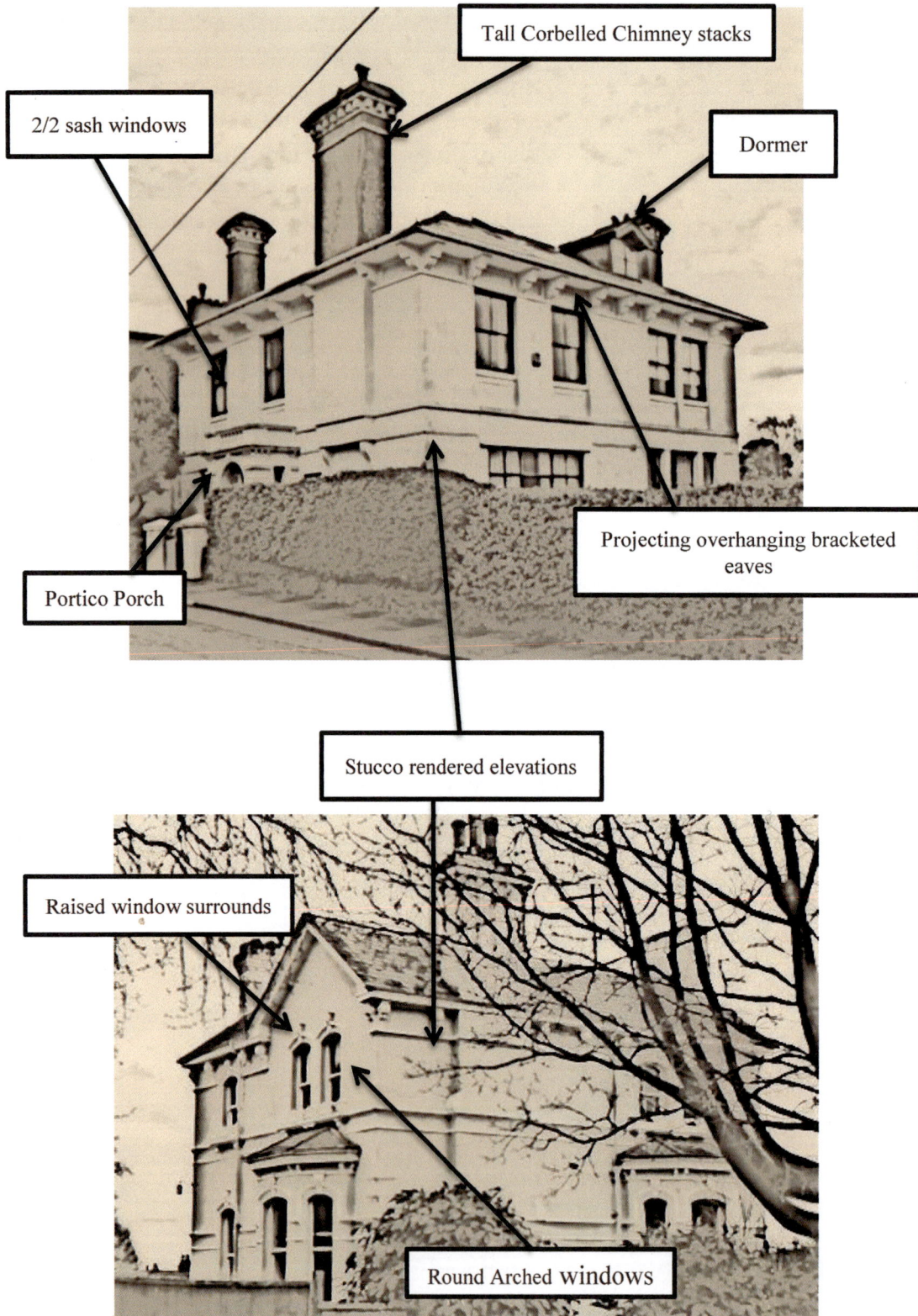

Tall Corbelled Chimney stacks

2/2 sash windows

Dormer

Projecting overhanging bracketed eaves

Portico Porch

Stucco rendered elevations

Raised window surrounds

Round Arched windows

Britains population doubled with the urban based proportion increasing from 54% in 1851 to 79% by 1911. The result was a massive expansion of towns to which the speculative builder responded building suburbs which were sharply delineated by class. Working class districts were built cheek-by-jowl with the collieries, mills and factories which provided employment for their inhabitants. In Malvern, in 1846, Edward Thomas Foleys' widow, Lady Emily Foley, held the manor till her death in 1900 and held a tight rein on the speculative builders.

The Foley lands stretched eastwards to the river (Severn) 3,000 acres, but there were a number of freehold properties islanded in its midst. The North side of Church street was owned by the Foleys. In 1846 180 acres of land was sold by the Mason estate who owned Southfield to the south of the Priory Gateway.(now Abbey Road) Regulations and clauses in conveyances of the plots stated that Villas should be detached or semi-detached and not sited 'opposite to or in parallel line with any other villa or residence'. Available building land owned by the Foleys had similar planning imposed. (Smith, 1964)

Without the arrival of Dr Gully to practice Hydropathy in Malvern with Dr Wilson back in the 1840s and 50s, Malvern would not have grown into a town and become an important major Victorian Spa of England by 1851. Along with Dr Grindod they brought their expertise in both physic and marketing and put Malvern on the international spa map. Many visitors came for the health cure and the fresh air on the Malvern Hills from London and the cities including many famous names including Dickens, Charles Darwin, Tennyson and Florence Nightingale.

'Hydropathy has taken possession of Malvern and peopled its houses...........labouring under ill health make it a place of fashionable resort' (Birmingham, n.d.)

'The Hydropathic establishments have contributed much to increase the prosperity of Malvern' (Directory, 1860)

Malvern Is unquestionably the principle seat of hydropathic practice, or "water treatment", in England. (J.B.Oddfish, 1863)

'Malvern grew with the success and popularity of hydropathy.... In 1842 there were 477 dwelling houses and a population of only 2768. Twenty years later there were six Hydropathic Establishments, 86 lodging houses, and the population had doubled. By the 1871 census the number of lodging houses had risen to 207. At the height of the season, they were said to be over 2000 visitors at any one time; the majority born in Britain, the rest hailed from the Empire, except for a few from Europe, the birthplace of spas.... Most of the large Victorian lodging houses were built by the 1850s. The Malvern Advertiser printed visitors' lists; these contained the names of houses which remain unchanged today... Also, the names of the springs and hills around Graffenburg were given to their counterparts on the Malvern's thus reinforcing the concept of a Graffenburg in England... Patients had the 9 miles into the hills to walk over.. (WindsorHarcup, 2010 .97)

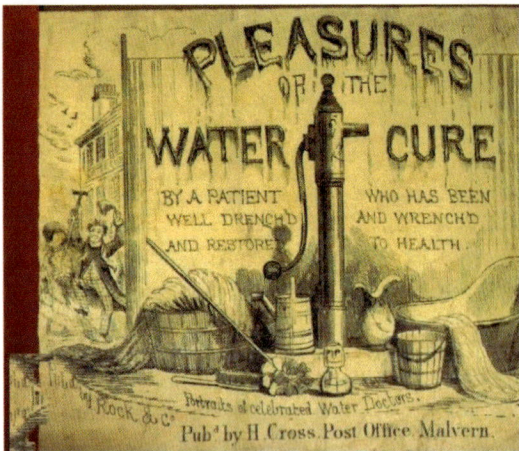

Fig 31 Pleasures of the Water Cure

However by the late Victorian period Hydropathy became less fashionable but Malvern still remained a place to visit.

The Architecture of the time was a true 'Battle of the Styles' so this guide will discuss the Classical and Gothic Revival in two Sections.

5.2 The Villa Style

The Italianate Revival was started by Nash and inspired by Osborne House, Queen Victorias Isle of Wight Country retreat. It became fashionable for classical symmetrical styles, square, 'belvedere' towers, deep projecting eaves, roof balustrades and round arched windows. A large middle class villa of the 1850s or 1860s could contain twelve rooms or more with separate family and service areas. Highly elaborate stucco remained popular when good stone was not available but lost favour in the 1860s with the Gothic Revival style (See Victorian Gothic Section 6) Fine stucco examples can be seen on the Holland Park Estate in West London, built by William and Francis Radford between 1860 and 1879. There are some similarities to these villas, albeit on a smaller scale, in Malvern.

5.3 Materials

Brick covered in lime stucco render or left uncovered but often decorated with stone or brick quoins. Building construction had changed little from the Georgian period for the domestic house-party walls in brick, internal walls lathe and plaster. Welsh slate was popular for roofing. Sash windows with the use of plate glass was used by the mid Victorian period

5.4 Materials used in Malvern in relation to style.

Stucco pilasters, stucco entablatures, in some cases with stucco Corinthian pilasters, and other Italianate detail are abundant. Stucco-faced ground floor and basements, strings, (horizontal mouldings) parapet and architraves of stucco. Balustrades, Doric Porches, and large Bay windows

5.5 Malvern Architects

Unknown for Malverns Italianate styles of architecture but nearby Witley Court was remodelled in an Italianate style between 1854 and 1860 by the architect Samuel Whitfield Daukes, commissioned by the owner the first Earl of Dudley who encased the house in Bath stone. It is now in ruins due to a fire in 1937, but open to the public and owned by English Heritage

Fig 32 Witley Court 1850

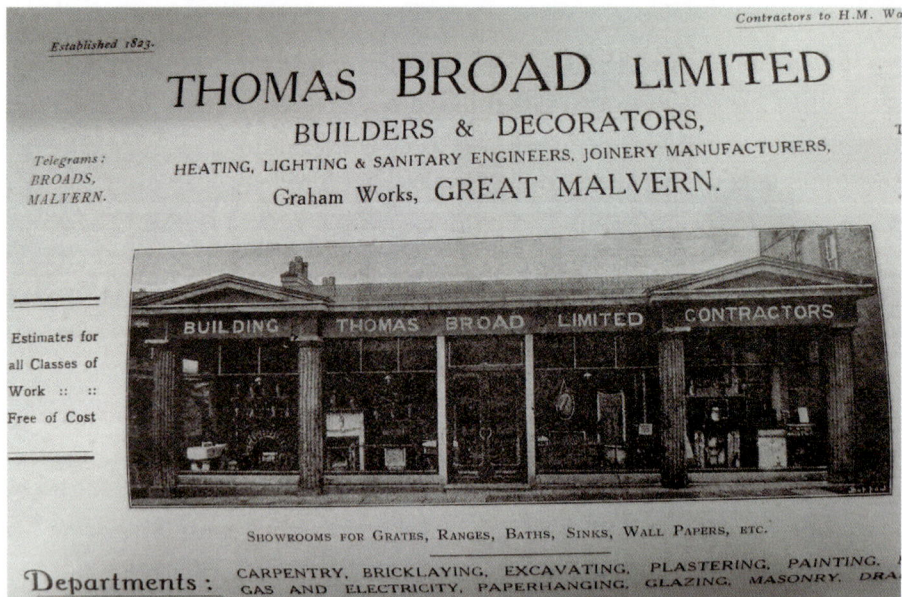

Fig 33 Thomas Broad Est 1832 Source: Stevens Annuals Directory 1920s

5.6 Architectural Appraisal and Notable Victorian Italianate Examples in Malvern

Photos: Author unless stated

Some notable buildings have been sadly lost in Malvern particularly during the 1960s and 70s. A few fine examples of Italianate style Villas were demolished like St Cuthberts, later used as a School, like so many large Malvern Boarding Houses or Villas. Others fortunately were listed in 1979 and here are a few notable Listed Villas in this style.

Fig 34 Italianate Examples

[1] Graham Road

[2]Graham Road

These two GD II Listed Villas [1 & 2] stucco rendered Villas are of the plainer style Whereas[3] GD II Listed Montrose Hotel displays stucco pediments
The sun room over the portico porch having been added by local architect Troyte Griffith at a much later date[3]

[4]GD II Listed 35 Buckingham House Graham Road & 33 Clanmere with porticos with flat entablature and blocking course on fluted Ionic columns. Ornamental cast-iron balconies to 1st floor windows

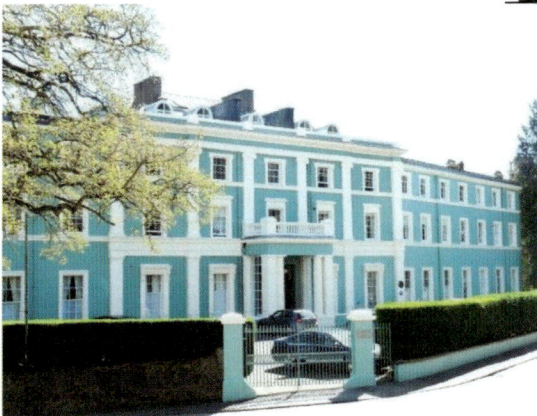

[5]Park View 33 Abbey Road Circa 1845. GD II Listed. Formerly Priessnitz House, built for Dr James Wilson as the 1st and one of the last large-scale hydropathic establishment in Malvern. The advertisement below before WW1 advertises Large Garden, Level Tennis and Croquet Lawns. Bathing Establishment, Douches, Packs, Sprays, Brine, Electric Light, Motor Excursions

Source: Malvern Library Archive Directories

Here we have one of Malverns three Italianate Towers. [6] Only Aldwyn Tower [6] is GD II listed. The third version was built in 2013/14 (See Section 12)

Source: Malvern Library Archive Directories

Fig 35 Notable unlisted Italianate Buildings

[1]Link Tower, Somers Road is remarkably similar to Aldwyn Tower above, and is undoubtedly by the same Architect Henry Day. Link Tower also has attached the later Raglan House also unlisted on the same site

Raglan House [2]with stucco basement, use of bricks and stucco quoins. A fine arched portico entrance[2]. Below[3] [4]two fine villas on Worcester Road [3] and [4 Ashlar stucco to ground floor to look like stone, two Doric columns at entrance. Ashlar stucco on [4] ground floor and two projecting bay windows
Two more highly decorated stucco Villas [5 &6] [Avenue Road and Albert Road South]

The following two Villas have a remarkable similarity. One is in the centre of town Chartwell House[7] and the other is much larger and further away[8](Abbey Road) Both have decorative brackets at eaves, natural coloured stucco render. Chimneys on [8] are particularly fine and decorated with stucco and Roman cement.

These two Villas are either end of town,[9] on Cowleigh Road and Linden Lea [10] in the centre of Great Malvern. Both are examples of Mid C19 Stucco Classical Villas with rusticated stucco and doric porches. One of the three curved terraces of Lansdowne Crescent [11] and a very italianate Villa [12] with large chimney stacks . Ashfield[13] is one of the few stone faced villas in this style.

Finally [14] BRAYS Worcester Road, the Italianate Department Store.

Fig 36. Victorian Gothic House Parts
Buildings from Malvern Source: Author

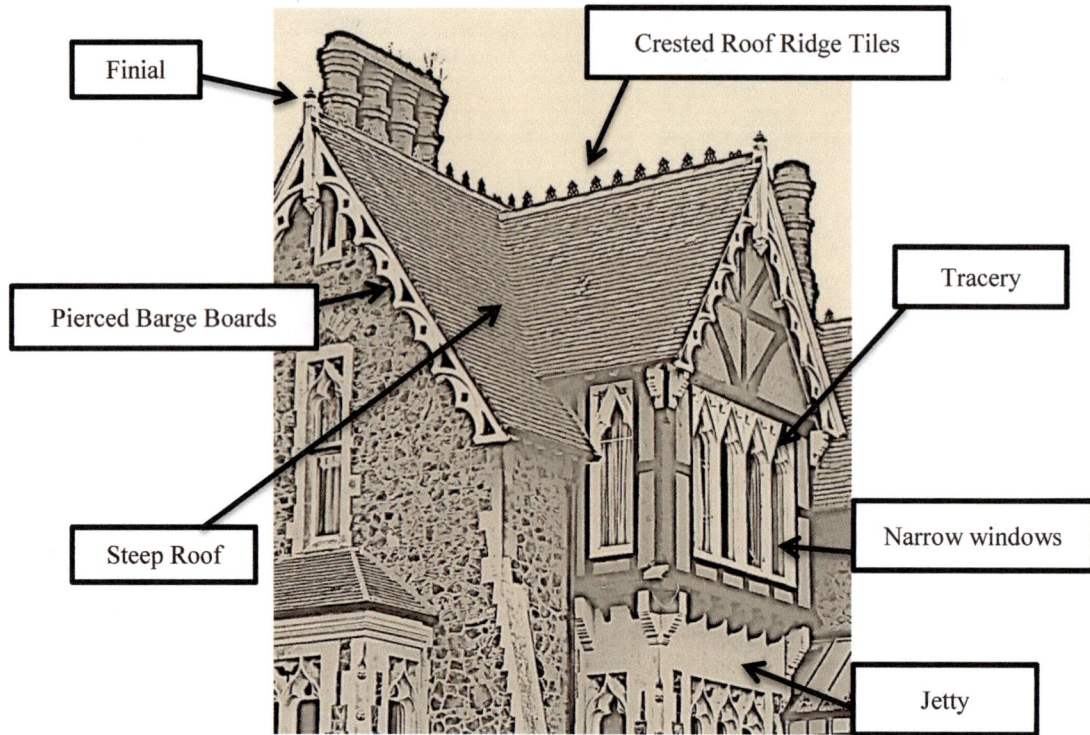

Finial

Crested Roof Ridge Tiles

Pierced Barge Boards

Tracery

Steep Roof

Narrow windows

Jetty

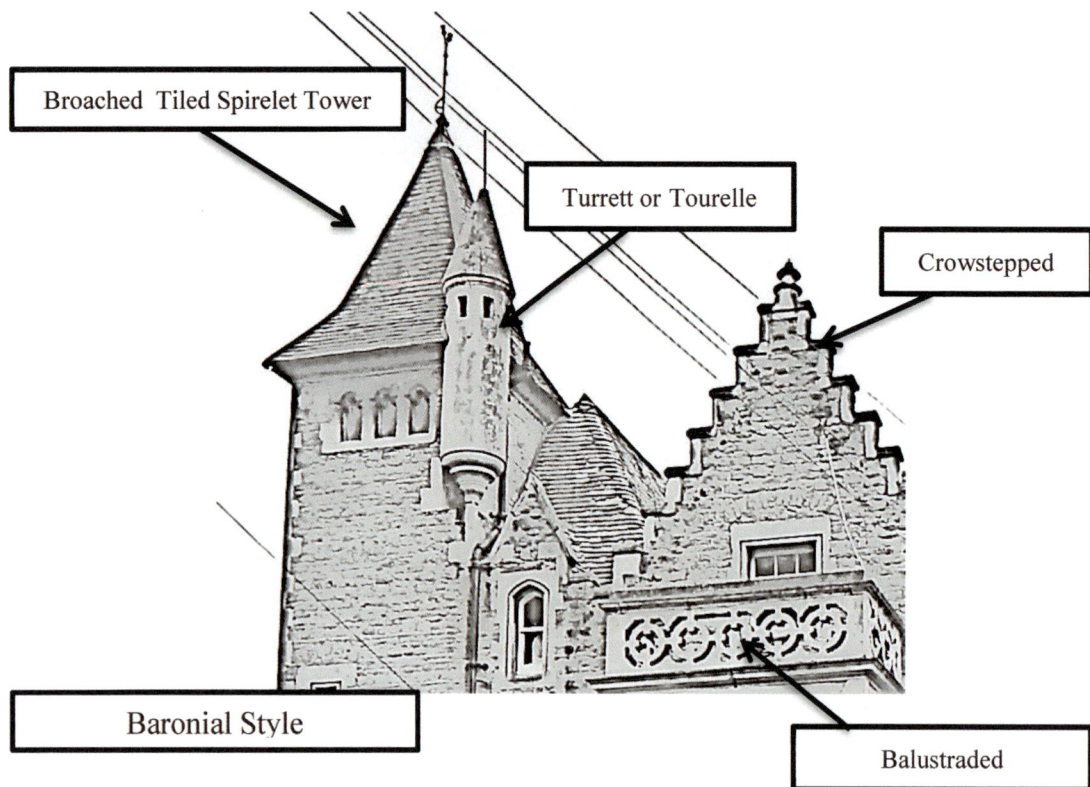

Broached Tiled Spirelet Tower

Turrett or Tourelle

Crowstepped

Baronial Style

Balustraded

6.1 Historical Note/Context

The Victorian era was one of great engineering a good example being the incredible Crystal Palace in London that housed the 1851 Exhibition, the Railway Stations and Hotels, Viaducts and Bridges. (Avery, 2003) Many of these took on the Gothic style like at St Pancras Station London. It was also a remarkable period of Church building that revived the Anglican Church and the Gothic style used had an influence on the architects for house building.

6.2 The Style

'The most important public building in England was to be Gothic' (Clark, 1950) The Houses of Parliament. The Gothic Revival divides itself very clearly into two periods, the first the Picturesque, the Houses of Parliament standing midway. 'By 1850 the triumph of Gothic in Church building was practically complete but ordinary man was not prepared for its application to other buildings.' (Clark, 1950)'Two men were responsible for converting England to secular Gothic, Ruskin and Gilbert Scott. Mullioned windows, pointed arches and high pitched roofs. Gilbert Scott wrote Domestic Architecture. 'we can never forget the Gothic Revival. It changed the face of England, building and restoring churches all over the countryside, and filling our towns with Gothic banks and grocers. Gothic Lodging-houses and insurance companies, Gothic everything, from a town hall down to a slum public house....There cannot be a main street in England quite untouched by the Revival' (Clark, 1950.294) The Gothic style gave way to the French Gothic, Italian Gothic and French Renaissance. Also 'The Castle Style' that included the Scottish Baronial style that came across the border to England. (Avery, 2003)An array of pointed arches, a revival of the Medieval arch, fashionable red brick, towers and turrets, (often placed at the end of a terrace or detached house),diaper patterns (exposed brick with patterns of different colours)and stone dressings, trefoils and quatrefoils, steep pitched roofs, gables, decorated bargeboards, ridge tiles and finials and tall narrow windows.

6.3 Materials

There was an Increase in the use of iron and steel for industrial and commercial building. (Clarke, 2014) For Domestic buildings:- stone or bricks or mixture of both. Polychrome decoration (different coloured bricks) roofs of slate or tiles often of different colours.

6.4 Materials used in Malvern in relation to style.

The Malvern Gothic style was influenced by the trends in London and other cities. Many of the visitors who came to Malvern for Hydrotherapy during the 1850's were from the fashionable areas of London and also many came from America for the water cure. They may well have commissioned many of the Gothic styles for many of the Villas found in Malvern and most certainly the Hydropathic Doctors commissioned Architects to follow the trendy style of the time for their Hydrotherapy Hotels. A good example is the French Gothic Elmslie 'Imperial Hotel '[Fig39 now a school] the Baronial Scottish style by SS Teulon, the Tudor Hotel on Wells Road and 'Elmsdale' on Abbey Road . Also typical the American Gothic style particularly used for bargeboards [Fig 37]Materials used were variety; red brick with diaper patterns, stone and stone dressings and carvings (evident by The Worcester stone mason -William Forsyth, [See Fig 40] Intricate carved wood for pierced bargeboards and finials and of course the more vernacular use of local Malvern stone to face buildings giving a crazy paving look, unique and only found in Malvern.

Malvern Builders; *One Leading Local Builder was George McCann. Sources of building materials came from local stone quarries, countless claypits and lime kilns. There were large brick works at Pixham, Rhydd, Mathon and Colwall. Malvern Link was centre of brickmaking with five works- Interfields, Spring Lane and Belmont. (Smith, 1964)*

Fig 37. Pierced Bargeboards popular in American Gothic Architecture seen here on a house in Malvern. It is one of many houses in Malvern that have pierced bargeboards.

6.5 Malvern Architects

George Edmund Street came to Malvern and designed St Peters Church in Cowleigh and St James in West Malvern, Gilbert Scott was also in Malvern for the restoration work on the Priory, the North door and possibly the Gatehouse,(See 2.1) Pugin was also nearby in the 1870s for the additions he made to Stanbrook Abbey Chapel and Cloisters, Charles F Hansom of Clifton for Malvern College and the School house in 1864 .The later Victorian Malvern College Chapel of 1897-99 by Sir A Blomfield is also in a Gothic style.

The Architects responsible that are known about for the Hydrotherapy Establishments and domestic Villas in Malvern are S.S. Teulon. E.W. Elmslie, and partners Haddon and Franey and later William Henman FRIBA.

6.6 E.W.Elmslie 1818-1889

His best known works in Malvern are the Great Malvern Station, a GD II Listed Building, and the Imperial Hotel now Malvern St James School on Avenue Road, also a GD II Listed Building. Recently in 2012 'The Grove', a villa originally designed for Dr Archibald Weir was also designated GDII. E.W.Elmslie, born in 1818, was in practise with Henry Haddon and Franey from Hereford. Elmslie also had an address in London. Elmslie designed nearby Whitbourne Hall in Worcester for Vinegar magnate Edward Bickerton Evans in about 1860 in a Greek Revival style but found his own distinctive style here in Malvern. Elmslie and partners designed many Churches around England particularly in Herefordshire DULAS, St. Peter (1864) Herefordshire, LLANWARNE, Christ Church (1862-1864) Herefordshire, ROWLSTONE, St.Peter (1865) Herefordshire, TUPSLEY, St. Paul (1864-1866) Herefordshire

Fig 38 Malvern Link Hotel by Elmslie (Demolished) Source: Postcard

Fig 39 Malvern St James School former Imperial Hotel by Elmslie Source:Author

6.7 Haddon Bros

The Haddon Brothers George and Henry Rockcliffe continued to practise after Elmslie left the area .Elmslie signed a debtors deed in late 1866, having dissolved his architectural partnership earlier that year. The Haddons are responsible for many of the Gothic style Villas in Malvern. William Forsyth, the Worcester Stone Mason, responsible for many of the intricate stone carvings found all around Malvern. In 1867 the Forsyths account books records carving a fireplace at 'The Grove' and for a Dr Weir in 1884/5 carving a Chimney piece for the Billiard Room, bosses, and spandrills.

William Henman FRIBA, worked on some chambers in Cornwall St. in Birmingham but his best known building in Birmingham is the General Hospital, for which he won a competition in 1882 in a neo-Jacobean design. Recently listed in 2012 was the Council Chamber, Albert Road, Aston, a local government building of 1880 by Henman. In Malvern William Henman is known to have designed 'The Skilts', Somers Road, but most notably The 1911 Community Hospital at Lansdowne Crescent commissioned by CW Dyson Perrins, Henman having already made additions to Dyson Perrins 'Davenham House' and additions at Malvern College (Pevsner, 2007) There may be further unknown attributed buildings by him.

6.9 Samuel Sanders Teulon 1812-1873

S.S Teulon designed 56 Churches but was also prolific for country houses. The best known in Malvern is GD II Listed 'The Tudor Hotel' on Wells Road, built for Dr Gully for Hydrotherapy. This was recently discovered to be by him by archive drawings at the RIBA (Pevsner, 2007) A useful source of information about this London born Architect can be found from his three times great nephew Alan Teulon in 'The Life and Work of Samuel Sanders Teulon, Victorian Architect'. (Teulon, 2009) and the RIBA collection, Pevsner Guides, and 'The Architectural Outsiders' by Kerry Downes, (Downes, 1985). Teulon is not mentioned in 'A Biographical Dictionary of British Architects 1600-1840', by Colvin. Samuel Sanders Teulon was for a long time derived and dismissed by Pevsner in the first Buildings of England Series. (Pevsner, 1951-74) Since then others have written about the mans genius.

"At Perry Hall for Lord Calthorpe in 1850, long since demolished but a very picturesque bridge was built over the moat. An even smaller staircase bridge in Malvern was almost certainly by Teulon. Dr Gully employed SST at Malvern to build a large house… One of my many Teulon enthusiast contacts discovered two unidentified perspective sketches of the front and the rear of the building in the RIBA drawings collection and immediately recognised them as what he knew as Tudor Hotel in Malvern. It was built about 1850 for Dr James Gully… Tudor house for the men was linked to Holyrood House for the women by a bridge."
"SST also built two houses for James Loftus Marsden, the first partner of Gully….
SST built Hardwicke house in 1851 which had a bath house in the rear of the property that is now a private house (Royds Lodge) Hardwicke house was demolished but nearby is the second house, Elmsdale, that still has a plaque with the initials JLM." (Teulon, 2009.71)

Royds Lodge, Hardwicke House (demolished) and Elmsdale on Abbey Road are now known and proven to be Teulon buildings but there are other possible Teulon buildings in Malvern. These are possibly 'Southbank' 47 Abbey Road and maybe Priors Croft Grange Road could also be a Teulon building as there is a remarkable similarity.
Teulon was well sort after at the time and had a very impressive client list;
Dukes of Bedford, Marlborough and St Albans, The marchioness of Londonderry, The Earls of Darnley, Ducey, Leicester, Radnor, Spencer, Stafford, and Yarborough. Countess Waldergrave, Lord's Calthorpe, Grovesnor and Northampton, Ladies Harriet Cooper, St John and Sarah Webster, Sirs Edward Brackenbury, Anthony Brown, Percy Burrell, Robert Jacob Buxton, Thomas Fowell Buxton and Henry Peyton, Prince Albert, Queen Victoria's Consort.
(Teulon, 2009)

Samual Teulon lived in the fashionable suburb of Hampstead in North London which was very fashionable and desirable in 1864. Others who lived in Hampstead then were George Gilbert Scott (another Malvern connection) Bodley and Teulons close friend and architect Ewan Christian .The book 'Architectural Outsiders' by Matthew Saunders has a complete chapter on Samuel Sanders Teulon and a List of Works on pages 218-226 taken from RIBA Sketchbooks 1 & 2. (Downes, 1985)

Fig 40 Some Elmslie Examples: The GDII Listed Great Malvern Station, Malvern St James former Imperial Hotel and recently 'The Grove', [now Elmslie House] on Avenue Road

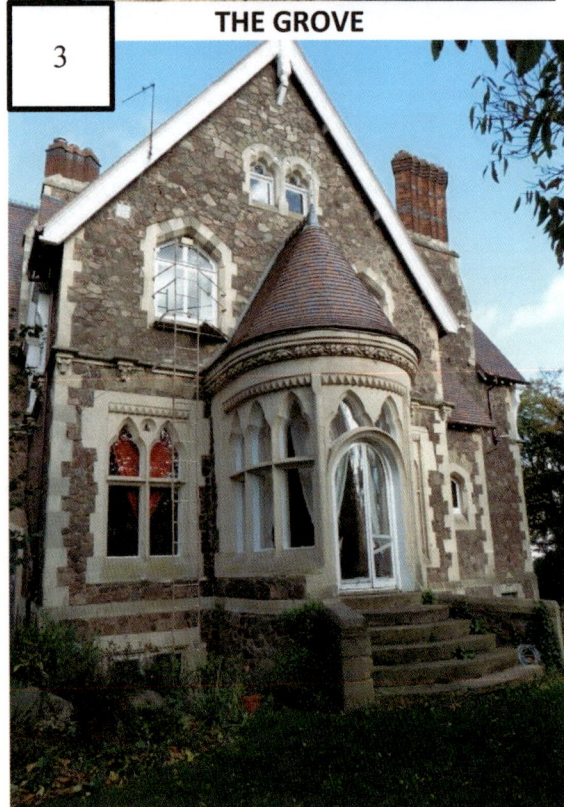

THE GROVE

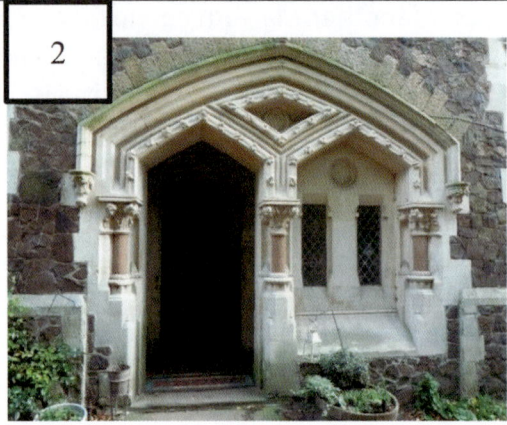

The Grove[1] intricate carvings around doorway[2]Fairy-tale gothic bow bay window and trefoil arched windows [3][5] Detail of Forsyths carving[4] and [5] with chevron lintels to windows

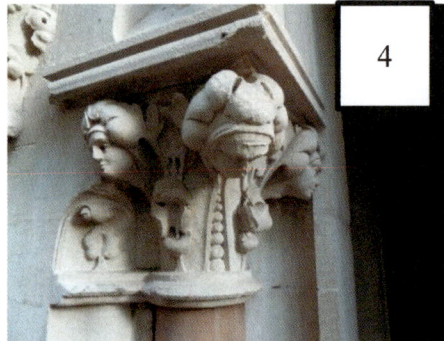

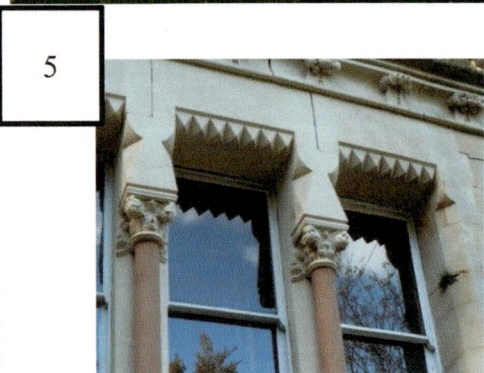

Fig 41   Unlisted and possible Elmslie Buildings.

Cotford Hotel [1]

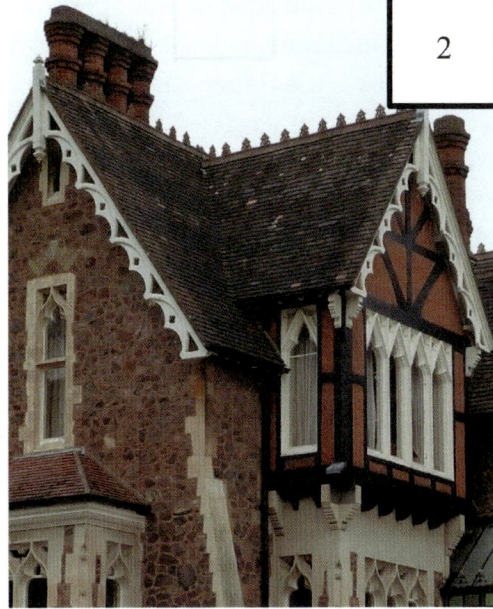

Cotford Hotel Graham Road [1/2]
'Best is the picturesque Cotford Hotel said to be 1851;dec details, pierced bargeboards, even a timber framed gable' (Alan Brooks, 2007)

Malvern Parish School[3] and 74 Stoberry & 72 The Lynches Albert Rd South use of brick

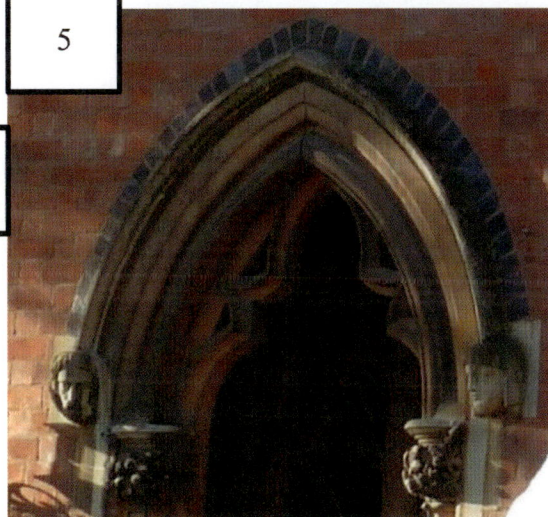

Source: Brian Iles Collection

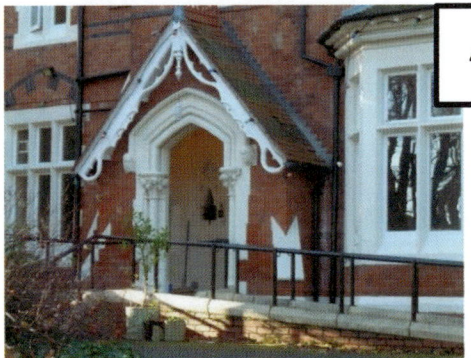

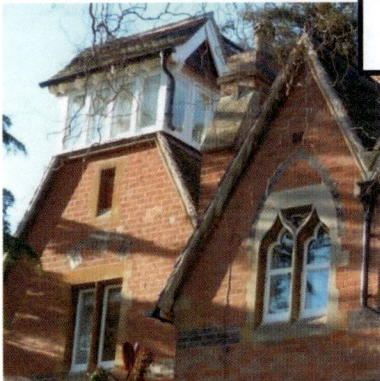

Carvings possibly by William Forsyth

The Haddon Bros

Fig 42   Listed Council House by Haddon Bros

The current Council House c1874 was thought to be previously an Elmslie building that was demolished, called 'the Priory', and has one remaining pillar.

Original Entrance c1860. The Priory Source: Brian Iles Collection

Pinnacles/turrets/trefoils. Faced in Cradley Stone with Bath stone dressings & carvings

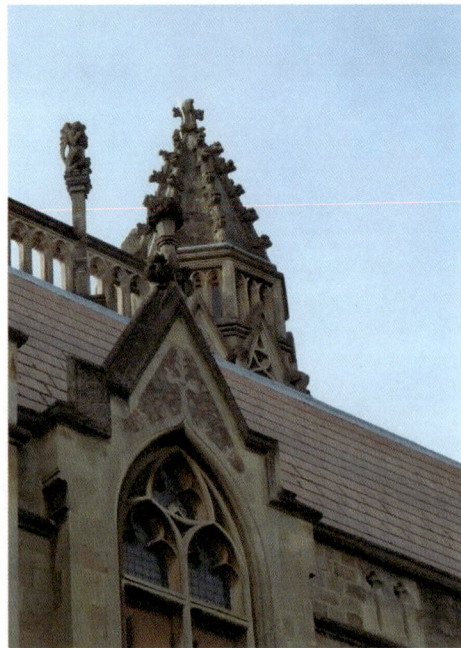

Fig43   Unlisted Haddon Bros Buildings of Note

1

2

The Gentlemans Club [1] Church Street

Batsford House [2]Avenue Road

Fig 44   Details on Batsford House

1

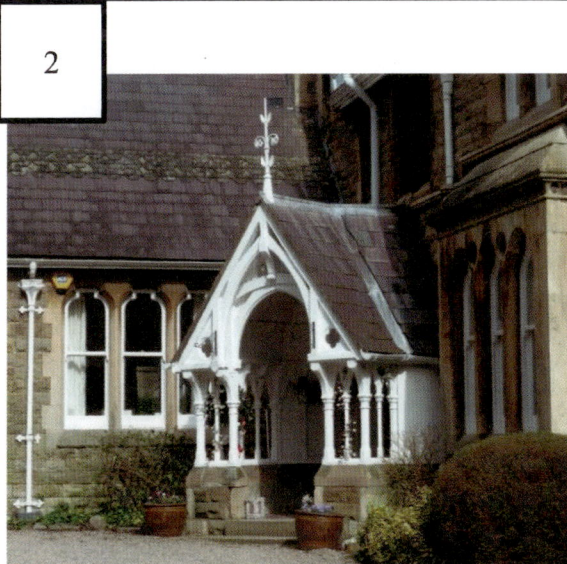
2

3

4

Victorian Gothic Lodge/Villa of c1870 built for the Speer family. Tall patterned brick chimneys[1]Angled timber porch[2]Carvings possibly by Forsyth[3]Ornate Bay[4]

Fig 45   Other Notable Haddon Bros unlisted Buildings

Lorne Lodge Sling "*patterned brick 1870 – 80 by Haddon*" (Alan Brooks, 2007) [1]
Haddons own house named 'Rockcliffe' with leaded tented roof on iron brackets[2]
Possibly by Haddon, Number 8 Manby Road [3]and 125 The Hollies[4] Worcs Road '*1879 no doubt by Haddon Bro*s' (Alan Brooks, 2007)
Polychromatic brickwork [4]
Possibly Haddon Bros ' Rockburn' on Victoria Road [5] Diaper string courses

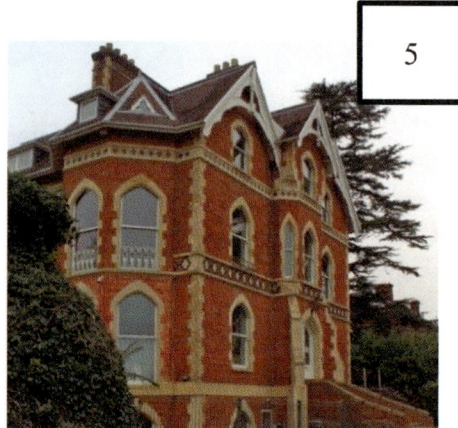

Fig 46 High Victorian Gothic
Out of the Teulon Buildings only Tudor Hotel (now Tudor Court) Wells Road [1] is listed.

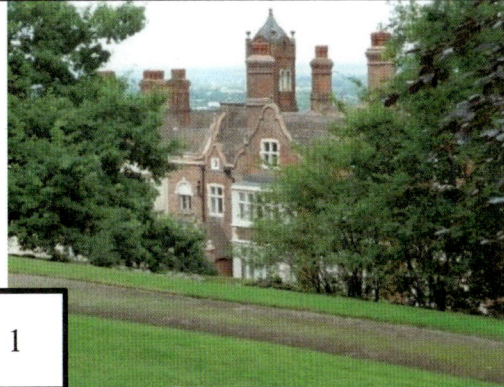

The following unlisted buildings have now been attributed to Teulon. Hardwicke House [2]was demolished [Malvern Gazette 1963] thought originally to be by Pugin [Brian Smith 1964] James Loften Marsden was a tenant until 1870s when Littleburys Directory has the house advertised as a Boarding House. Now Flats c1960 (Section 11) but Elmsdale survives[3] below and Royds Lodge too where the Turkish Baths were housed.

Hardwicke House — the original

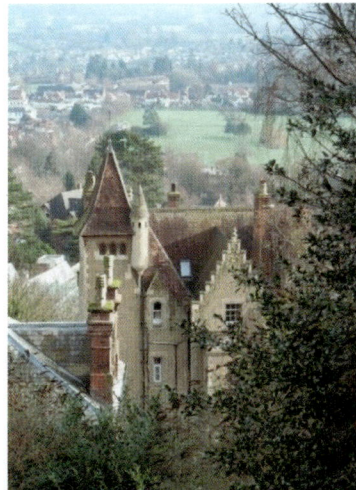

Elmsdale- Abbey Road Typical Scottish Baronial style.[4] Notice the fairytale turrents and castelleted parapets.[4] Unfortunately there is a large UPVC window in the front façade not shown here. There is a C19 RIBA Drawing on RIBA Website

Fig 47   Further notable High Victorian Gothic possibly some by Teulon

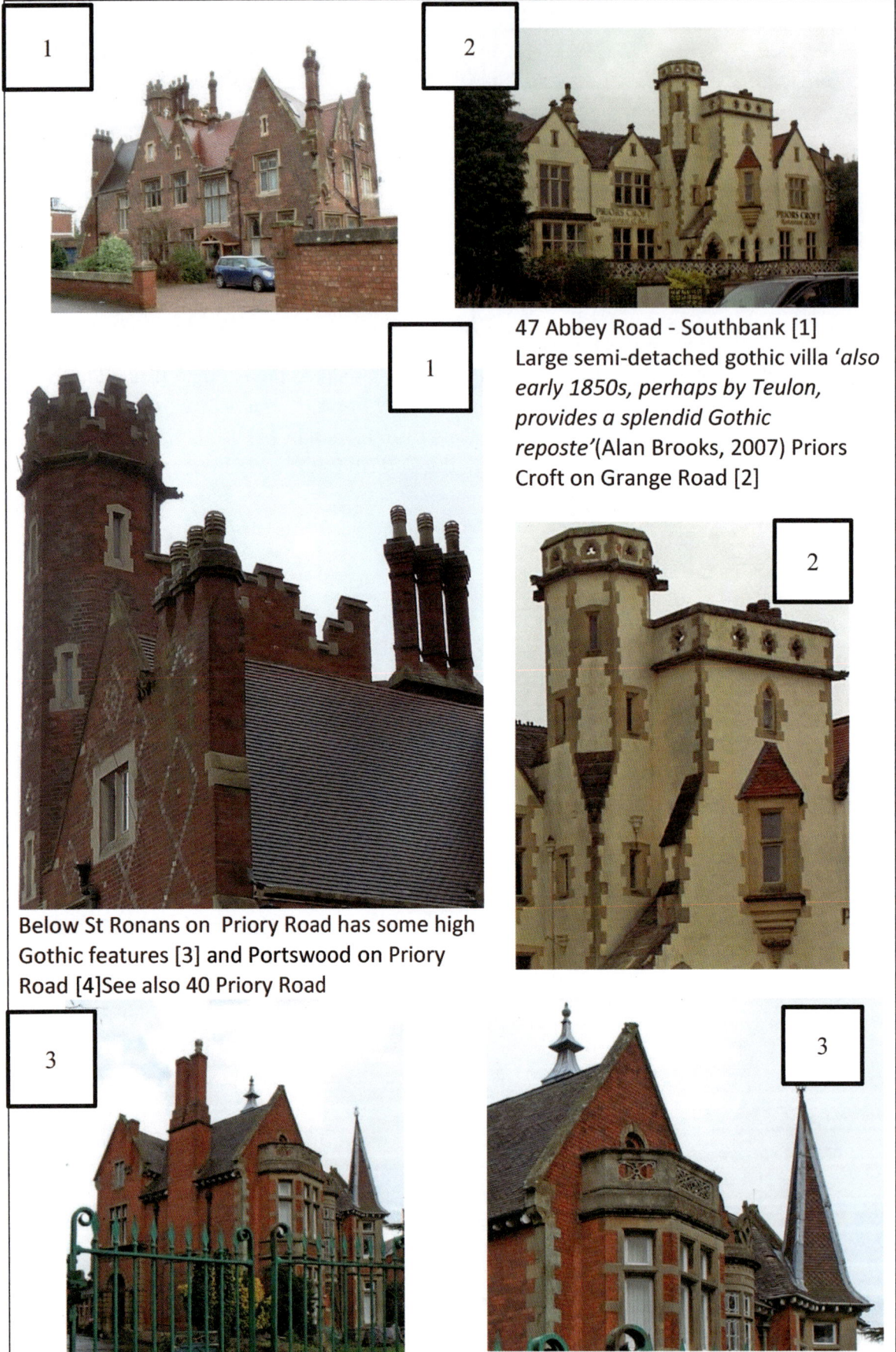

1

2

1

47 Abbey Road - Southbank [1]
Large semi-detached gothic villa *also early 1850s, perhaps by Teulon, provides a splendid Gothic reposte*(Alan Brooks, 2007) Priors Croft on Grange Road [2]

2

Below St Ronans on Priory Road has some high Gothic features [3] and Portswood on Priory Road [4]See also 40 Priory Road

3

3

Fig 48 'Malvern House' The Jacobean Mansion with Gothic overtones built for Dr Wilson in 1859 for Hydropathy. Architect unknown.

7. VICTORIAN MALVERN 1830-1900 - 1890s Victorian Styles

The 1890s Late Victorian Villa Classical style

7.1 The Villa Style

The Queen Anne Revival became vogue for individual town houses when the Gothic Revival and Italianate styles lost favour. As early as 1880 the so-called Queen Anne style of Norman Shaw was a menace to the Gothic party and by 1900 the Revival had ceased.

Workers houses were more uniform, rows of tightly packed terraces. The terraced house remained the builder's solution to the demand for cheap urban housing until the early 1900s. There was an increase use of decorative brickwork, and pre-fabricated terracotta by the 1890s.

7.2 Materials

For Domestic Buildings -red brick, sash windows, rubbed brickwork, bays and gables inspired by the Arts & Crafts movement and architects such as Norman Shaw, the Bedford Park Estate Chiswick London

(See also late Victorian examples in Malvern in Arts & Crafts, Section 8)

7.3 Materials used in Malvern in relation to style.

In Malvern there was less use of Malvern stone for the crazy paving style used and Cradley stone was used instead dressed with Bath Stone. A lot of 1890s building in Malvern still paid homage to the Gothic and most villas incorporated the odd trefoil or lancet window. Brick building continued. Most prevalent was the Arts and Crafts style from the 1880s and this is discussed in further detail in a separate section. [Section 8]

7.4 Malvern Architects

William Henman FRIBA. Others unknown but Haddon Bros and Broads Builders were still in Malvern and seemed to adapt to this 1880s-90s style.

Photos: Author and unless stated

Fig 49   Late Victorian styles

Imperial Terrace in 1885,Manby Road[1] National School by Haddons 1885 North Malvern Road [2], 18 and 20 Hornyold Ave[3] 1891 Promenade buildings Worcester Road [4]note the use of bricks and terracotta

Fig 50   Larger Late Victorian Villas

1 Avenue Road , [1] Tibberton House 1898[2] has a definite flavour of Norman Shaw about it. At 14 Avenue Road [3] and Fairhaven, Imperial Road [4] both these villas use Cradley stone with Bath stone dressings. Both houses have colour leaded mullion windows and the Trefoils have become circular.

Fig 51 Arts & Crafts House Parts
Buildings from Malvern Source: Author

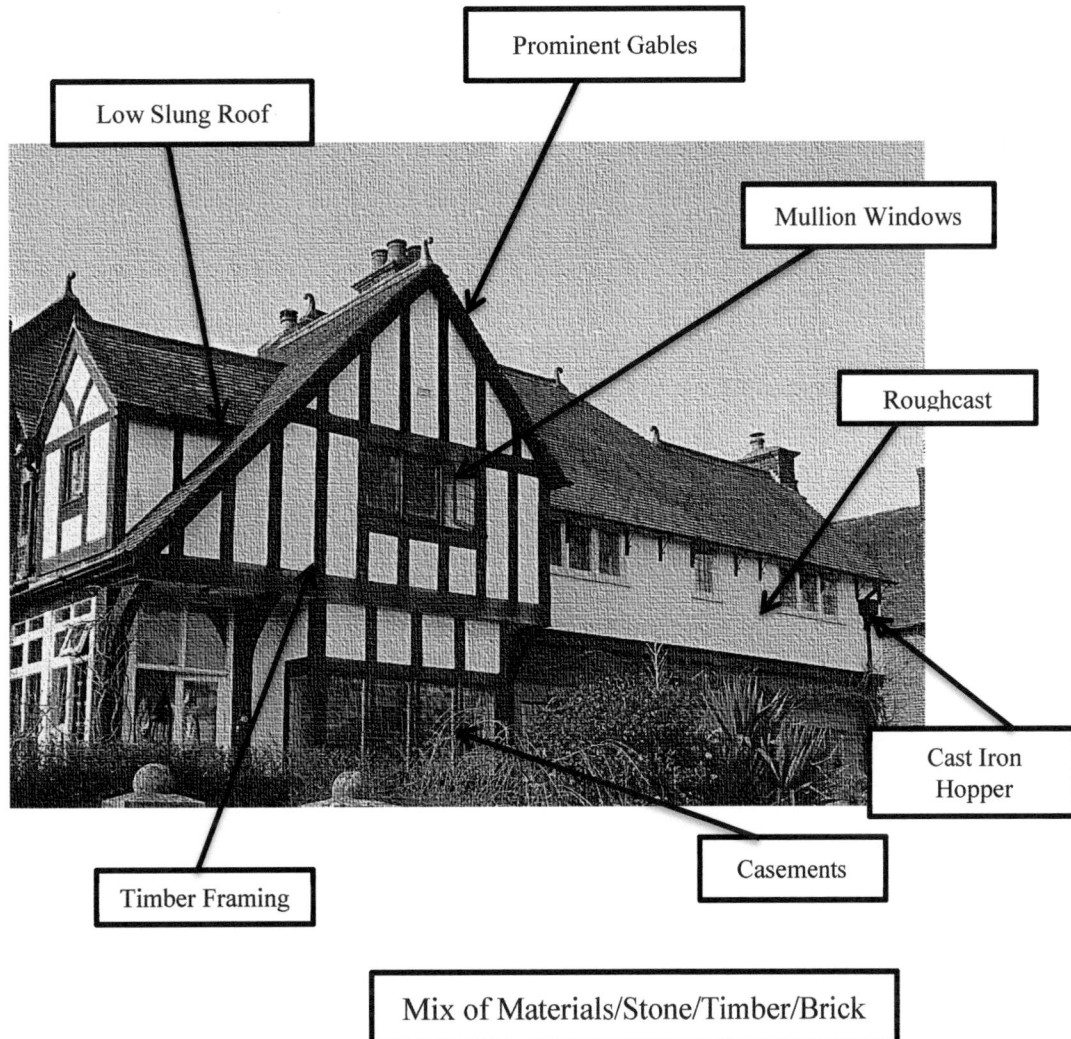

Prominent Gables

Low Slung Roof

Mullion Windows

Roughcast

Cast Iron Hopper

Casements

Timber Framing

Mix of Materials/Stone/Timber/Brick

8.1 Historical Note/Context

As Malvern grew as a wealthy Spa Town with its bespoke Villa residences some designs veered away from the Gothic style and were built in an Arts and Crafts style during the late Victorian period that lasted all the way through the Edwardian period until WW1

8.2 The Style

"There were a few rich manufacturers of armaments and very prosperous shopkeepers and bankers who could afford to build large private houses"... George Edmund Street chief draughtsman and Norman Shaw revolutionised English house building, especially when building country houses. "Friends from his days in Streets office like William Morris, Philip Webb designed the wall paper, curtains and furniture, Rosetti and Maddox Brown did the stained glass, William de Morgan tiled the fireplaces... He used redbrick, which had been unfashionable for a century and white wooden balconies" (Betjeman, 1972)

So what is an Arts and Crafts House? The author Trevor Yorke in his book *'Arts And Crafts House Styles'* sums up this style simply.

"Where traditional materials, techniques and styles in the local area (vernacular) were used to greater building of good quality and simple form....The architect is usually involved in the design of every detail... Buildings are usually referred to as such and were mainly erected from the 1870s to the early 1900s... Custom designed and handmade these houses were very expensive and usually reserved for the upper middle classes" (Yorke, 2011)

The fashion became widespread by the early 1900s to include terraces /semis and detached houses to the building of social housing schemes by speculative builders.
Malvern has some examples of these but the majority are custom designed detached villas. The origins of the Arts and Crafts movement was a reaction against the massed produced Victorian goods. The father figure of the Arts And Crafts movement was William Morris who concentrated on design, natural ingredients and traditional methods. The Arts and Crafts movement sometimes known as The Aesthetic Movement formed themselves into collectives/brotherhoods and became a big influence on architectural style

8.3 Materials

The architectural style of this period will often have a rendered exterior (roughcast) with walls broken up by exposed stonework/bricks, tall plain chimneys, mullion windows, bow windows, colourful patterned glass and low-slung tiled roofs. By the 1890s and 1900s timber framed gables, muscular bay windows and terracotta plaques were common. Later features had distinctive simplified forms and appeared modern with features like eyebrow dormer windows, angled wings and narrow slits. Inspiration came from the timber framed brick and stone cottages and former manor houses of the 16th and 17th century.
"On 18 September 1901, the Daily Mail featured an interview with Parker and Unwin about their book, the Art of building a home. Beneath the provocative headline "concerning the coming revolution in domestic architecture", appeared drawings with pricetags: a "£200 artisans cottage –, a £500 middle-class home – Unwins unbuilt design for his home in Derbyshire and a £10,000 country house....Both Letchworth and Hampstead brought the opportunity for individual houses in addition to the group designs juxtaposing the architecture of Parker and Unwin with that of their peers... The growing popularity of the Georgian revival: red brick, sash windows (Miller, 1992/2006)*Daily Mail 1901*

In evidence in Malvern are tiled and slate roofs. Roughcast elevations with a mix of materials, stone and brick; half-timbered gables; Bay windows with leaded lights often with coloured glass.

The builders of the early Malvern Arts and Crafts villas were probably more influenced by articles in 'Country Life Magazine' that first appeared in 1897 and the architects Edwin Lutyens and C.F.A Voysey who promoted building a weekend house larger than a cottage and the dream of a rural idyll. The architects of these similar types of villas are mostly unknown in Malvern and a lot of the smaller and semi-detached villas may have been built by speculative high class builders. However we do know that C.F.A Voysey (John Brandon-Jones, 1978) was in the vicinity and built Perry Croft on the other side of Malvern Hills. Voysey was one of the most talented and complete Arts and Crafts architects and designers. He set up his practice in 1882. His most productive stage of building came in the 1890s and early 1900s with a unique style, long sloping roofs, mullion windows and use of white roughcast. All features most popular with a wealthy clientele. Walter Tapper was also in Malvern (He designed The Church of the Ascension in Somers Park Road)
Other architects of the time were local architects Troyte Griffith, and Nevinson & Newton. All may have been influenced by established architects and perhaps by The Bournville Village, being so nearby. We know that Worcester based A. Hill Parker was architect of The Fountain Inn 1898[Fig 57] and later Malvernbury in 1907.[Fig56]The Birmingham based Crouch and Butler firm designed the Edwardian 1904 Queen Anne style Library in Malvern but were known more for their Arts and Crafts Villa styles. They did have clientele in Malvern.

Fig 52Perrycroft Colwall and Cobnash GD II Listed Source: Author

Cobnash Malvern Wells GDII Listed

1901, architect C F A Voyscy. Two storeys. Roughcast walls with stone dressings, hipped slate roof, roughcast chimney. First floor has 3 mullion windows of 2-4-2 lights, leaded glazing bars. Ground floor has windows of 2-5-2 lights, shaped cornices. Doorway with 4-centred arched head.

Fig 53 Late C19 Malvern Arts & Crafts Villas Photos:Author

Havenhurst ,21 Albert Park Road 1883. Havenhurst [1 & 2] displays typical Arts & Crafts features; fish scale clay tiles,tall corbelled chimney stacks, timber framed gables, an oak timber jettied porch to the front entrance. 32 Alexander Road [3]is another later style with flat roofed bow bays behind the tall hedge.

21 Somers Road (Havenhurst)   32 Alexander Rd c1890

The College Grove group [5] were all by local Architect Firm Nevinson & Newton and they too incorporate some Arts & Crafts style mixed with a little Gothic

26 Priory Road c1890[4] Another later Arts & Crafts influenced build

College Grove Group of four Villas [5]by Nevinson & Newton 1885 in an early Revival Arts and Crafts style. Mix of materials.

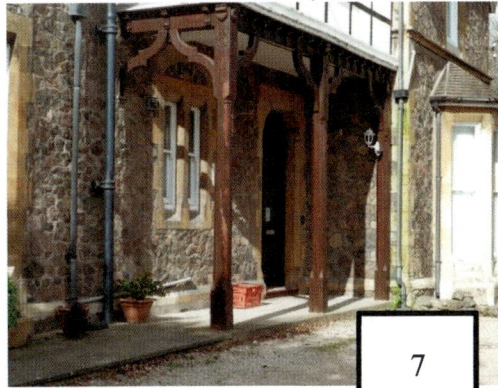

This Tibberton Road property [6] is very similar to Havenhurst [1 & 2]

2, Tibberton Road above[6] has 1883[date plaque] with timbered jetty over doorway, tall chimney stacks and timber framing to gables

2, Tibberton Road, Porch. These details are also found at Havenhurst on Somers Road [1&2]

1, Wilton Road (Wilton Place) [8] corner site. 1880 has a date plaque and carved stone sunflower (aesthetic movement) above ground floor bay window

Sunflower design bay window at 1 Wilton Place. [9]These sunflowers are found on gates and railings around Malvern (See Edwardian Section 9)

This villa on Wilton Road [8 &9] is reminiscent of buildings by Norman Shaw. Note the carved design below the upper window

Fig 54 Garden City influence on Moorlands road
Gardiners (six) Cottages on Moorlands Road built for estate workers at 'Davenham House' home to the Dyson Perrins family of Worcester Sauce fame and Worcester Porcelain. Gardiners Cottages were built sometime after the 1905 2nd Edition Ordnance Survey Map

The Area around Somers Road/Albert Park Road.

There was little built here in 1885. By 1908 a group of Arts & Crafts semi-detached villas were built. [Source the 1920s Ordnance Survey Map.]

Fig 55 Later C1900-14 Malvern Edwardian Arts & Crafts on Somers Road/Albert Park
Photos: Author

1

15/17 Somers Road c1908

Group of 1908 Arts and Crafts houses in Somers Road. All semi-detached probably built by speculative builders/local architects, all featuring typical designs See [1] and [2] recessed doors within porches, stained coloured glass in doors, leaded lights to bay windows. 15/17 Somers Road are bowed.[1 & 2] 25, Albert Park Road has two storey bowed bays[5 & 6] with added Dutch style gables and arched doorways

Original front doors with coloured patterned glass. Note the detailing; wrought iron brackets to cast iron guttering at 23 Albert Park Rd [3 &4]. This house also has buttresses.

2

3

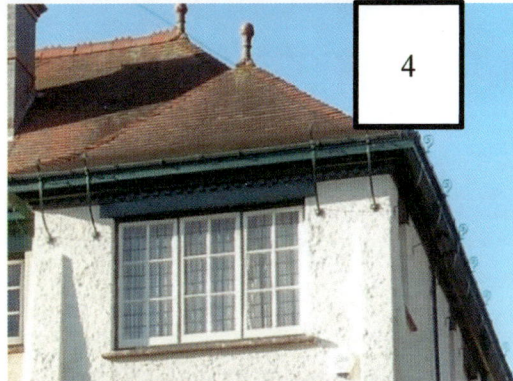

4

5

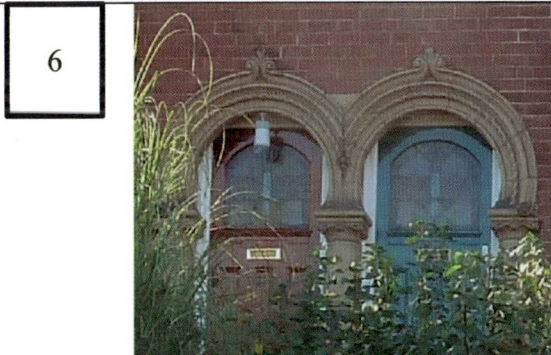

6

Twin porches and coloured door glass

A Triangular Oriel bay window feature at 29 Albert Park Road [7] with timber framing to gables and a wide recessed porch.

[8] Local architect Troyte Griffith is thought to have designed 145-147 Worcester Road ;semi-detached Villa with roughcast elevations 1903 [8]

A further group by Architects Crouch & Butler can be found in Woodshears Road and Court Road. [9]. All have Clay tiled pitched and gabled roofs with curled finials; typical Arts and Crafts wrought iron brackets at eaves and cast-iron hoppers.

29 Albert Park Road

145-147 Worcester Road

Bay at The Gables 92 Court Road

The Group of houses by Architects Crouch & Butler 1898-9 south of Oak Lodge on Woodshears Road did not exist In 1885. [Source 1885 1st Edition Ordnance Survey map.] The 1905 2nd Edition Ordnance map shows this group of buildings.They have been built along with Woodshears Road itself passing under the bridge to Court Road.

Fig 56 Sub-Voysey style in Malvern Photos: Author

This is a the 1907 Sub Voysey house called, Malvernbury, [1 & 2] Abbey Road. It was at risk of collapse in 2014. Note the eyebrow window detail and roughcast plain chimney stacks. A two and a half storey detached building designed in the Arts & Craft style in 1907. The Architect was Alfred Hill Parker, Worcester. Built as a private residence later becoming a school and a Nursing Home (Pevsner, 2007) Currently under renovation unfortunately with many details now lost including the Westmorland Slate roof tiles.

Eyebrow detail at Malvern bury, Abbey Road

Number 3 St Peters Road with low slung roofs and balconies [3]

6, St Peters Road,[4] known to be Crouch & Butlers work.(Title Deeds and Plans)

5

6

26 Peachfield 1904, has date on gable end. This house is outside the Great Malvern area but has been included in the Appraisal as a fine example of an Arts & Crafts house in the Malvern Wells area.[5 & 7]

1909 'Greyroofs', Peachfield Road. Architect Troyte Griffith (Pevsner, 2007)also outside the area but included as another fine example [6] *Built for a wealthy German Count who lived in London with his English wife and family before moving to Malvern* (Hardie, 2012)

7

26, Peachfield Rd-Note the Fleur de Lys and 1904 on gable, another tall plain roughcast chimney stack typical of Arts & Crafts styling.

Two Churches and one Church Hall were commissioned and built in the Arts & Crafts style in the Edwardian period 1901-14. The Church of the Ascension Somers Park Road in 1903 [2] by Architect Walter Tapper, is GD II listed and outside the Great Malvern Survey area, The Wyche Free Church 1910 at the Wyche, Jubilee Drive [1] designed by Harold Scott of Birmingham, (later better known as a cinema architect) was opened in 1911 (Dixon, 2011) is also outside the Survey area. The Church Hall at Holy Trinity Church is in the Survey Area. Built in 1910,Trinity Hall, North East, by Architect H.Percy Smith, 1910 – 11,[3] roughcast above brick, gabled projections, buttresses rising into the roof, small domed louvre (Alan Brooks, 2007). Only Perrycroft and Tappers Church are listed from all the Arts & Crafts buildings mentioned in this whole section as this type of Architecture in the 1970s was seen as not very important. 'Perrycroft' and Ascension Church have now been nationally recognised and listed more recently.

Fig 57 Church building in Arts & Crafts style Photos: Author

'Mr J. W. Wilson and his wife, who lived further down Jubilee Drive at "Perrycroft", a large new house recently designed by the celebrated architect, C. F. A. Voysey. Perhaps it is only coincidence but the Wyche FreeChurch, with its domestic scale, prominent buttresses and roughcast walls, is distinctly "Voysey-esqe" in character (Dixon, 2011)

Fig 58 Edwardian House Parts
Buildings from Malvern Source: Author

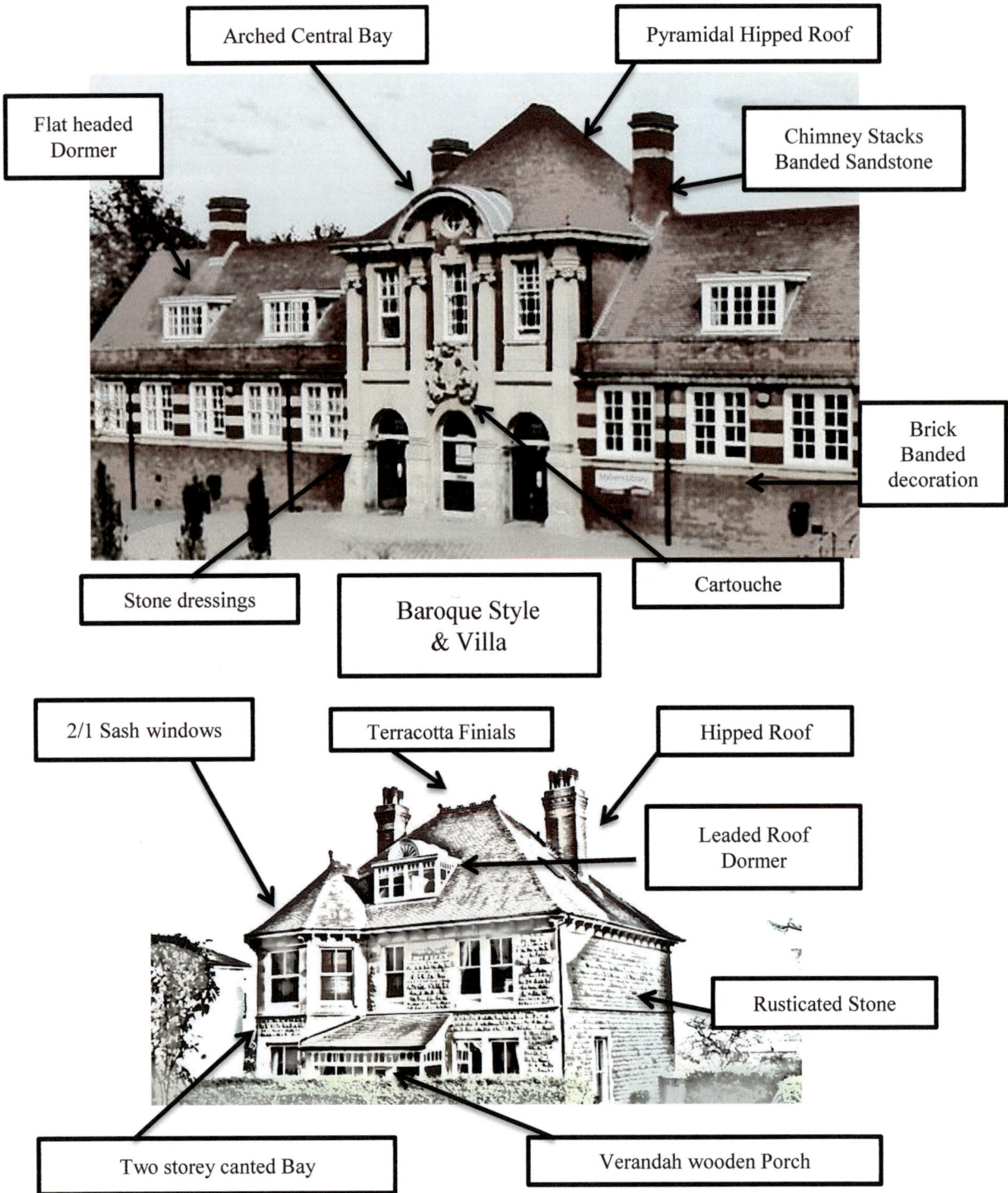

Arched Central Bay

Pyramidal Hipped Roof

Flat headed Dormer

Chimney Stacks Banded Sandstone

Brick Banded decoration

Stone dressings

Baroque Style & Villa

Cartouche

2/1 Sash windows

Terracotta Finials

Hipped Roof

Leaded Roof Dormer

Rusticated Stone

Two storey canted Bay

Verandah wooden Porch

1901 marked Edwards VII succession to the throne, Malvern tank gained a clock and Malvern gained a new benefactor as Lady Foley had died in 1900. The manor passed to her grandson Sir Henry Foley Lambert, Bart.

CW Dyson Perrins gave generously to the town, the Library in 1906 with funds by Andrew Carnegie and a new hospital that opened in 1911 [See fig 65], and he commissioned new pews for Holy Trinity Church in 1909. The Edwardian period saw the sale of the Foley Estate in 1910 and later after WW1 the Hornyold Estate in 1919. Sir Henry Foley Grey of the Lodge disposed of 1,365 acres below the railway from the Link End Farm and Pickersleigh Court, Moat Court, Grove House and Court Farm. In the Foley sale catalogues special emphasis was laid on the attraction of the houses and building plots to Birmingham businessmen. *"The Horny Old sale was even bigger, it included Tank and West Malvern quarries and property throughout Newtown and North Malvern"* (Smith, 1964.252) The real innovations of the age were the telephone, electricity (Malverns electricity works at Sherrard's green in 1904) and the motorcar. At Malvern Link TC Santler made the first motorcar in Britain in 1887 – 9 while HFS Morgan began making Morgans in 1910. In 1898 HG Burston of Newtown manufactured a steam motor and the number of cars encouraged the earliest of garages...... *A large portion of driving licences were taken out by Malvern residents in 1904 compared with the rest of the country* (Smith, 1964.253)

The exterior style of housing was dominated by the earlier work of revival architects like Norman Shaw and the Arts and Crafts movement. Classical styles became fashionable mainly for mansions and public buildings but a revival of early 18th-century houses known as Neo Georgian began to appear too. In towns there was a cross between "Dutch" and "Queen Anne" with red bricks and white stone dressings and domes on roofs. In the country mock Tudor maintained its popularity. After 1900 speculative builders were paying attention to designs by Voysey, Lutyens and others. Other aspects of detailed treatment between 1901 and 1911 reflected the increasing mechanisation of production of building materials for example terracotta and faience and the abundance of cheap labour.

Schools in the provinces became the responsibility of the local councils and local councils had powers to raise money from rates for building works .This gave work to many provincial architects; Libraries, Art Galleries, Police and Fire Stations, Public Baths, Generating Stations to Tenements and Workers Cottages. (See Arts & Crafts Section 8)
A new building type, The Telephone Exchange came into being and some distinguished examples were designed by Leonard Stokes, President of the R IBA from 1910 to 1912. Also new were the London Underground railway buildings by C. Stanley Peach.
Leisure activities began to flourish and the first modern covered football stands appeared in Edwardian times and working-class seaside resorts like at Blackpool with its Pier Tower and Ferris wheel. The Edwardian architect was extremely fortunate professionally and the need for many new buildings in a variety of different types must have provided stimulating challenges (Fellows, 1995)

9.3 Materials

Redbrick, pebble dashed/roughcast walls, left unpainted or limewashed, mock timber gables, hanging red tiles and terracotta decoration inspired by the Arts and Crafts movement; handles, tiles and stained glass, a revival of wrought iron was also popular at the time. Cast-iron was now almost universal for rainwater downpipes and hopper heads and there was an increase use of faience, (glazed terracotta.)

Even quite modest Edwardian terraced houses often displayed a good deal of painted woodwork, framing porches and complex patterns of glazing bars to windows. Houses frequently had balconies and verandas and elaborate wooden balustrades. (Johnson, 2006)

9.4   Materials used in Malvern in relation to style.

For Domestic Housing; Redbrick, roughcast /pebble dashed walls, mock timber gables, hanging red tiles and terracotta decoration; balconies and verandas and elaborate wooden balustrades. For the Municipal buildings stone or red bricks with white stone dressings and terracotta were used. For Mass produced terrace houses, the speculative builder added details from various sources including the Arts & Crafts style, typical of early 1900s. Rendered first floors, timber framed gables, muscular bow windows and terracotta plaques.

9.5 Malvern Architects

Not all buildings can be attributed to particular Architects and most were probably built by high class speculative building firms but some Architects are known for example William Henman for The Hospital on Lansdowne Crescent, Malvern College Gymnasium (now Rogers Theatre) The Radnor House extensions, Malvern College Boarding House, and The Bromsgrove Guild for the Gates at Davenham, Henry A Crouch, the Library 1906, and Albert C Baker for Portland House Church Street in 1907. (Pevsner, Alan Brooks and Nicolas, 2007)

Of all the buildings in this section from the Edwardian period only The Water Tower [1] and Library [3] are GD II Listed.

Fig 59 Edwardian Municipal Buildings Photos: Author

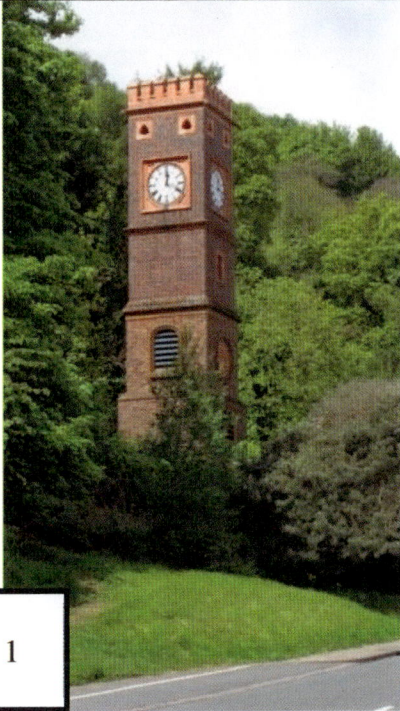

Water Tower North Malvern Road in brick and red terracotta, with clock, erected 1901.The Water Tower

Somers Park School, Church Road (detail) 1908-9 is an example of Local Council building (outside current Survey but worth noting)

1904 Malvern Library, Graham Road LISTED 14 June 2012 designed by Henry A Crouch in a loosely Baroque style and built by James Herbert

1

2

The Fountain Stores/Inn Court Road [1&2] just on the cusp 1898 by A.Hill Parker from Worcester. *Former Fountain Inn by A.Hill Parker 1898;roughcast brick terracotta trim, wide porch on timber columns* (Pevsner, Alan Brooks and Nicolas, 2007)

Fig 60 The Fountain Stores Court Road Photo:Author

Fig 61 Gymnasium, Malvern College detail (Now Rogers Theatre). Henman 1907-8
Photo: Author Note coloured glass leaded windows

Exchange Buildings- *'Exchanges were purpose-built structures devoted to commercial activity, somewhere for traders to display their wares, for customers to gather, for business negotiations to take place, and so forth – in many ways they were also the prototype for office building'* (English Heritage, April 2011)

Fig 62 Commercial Buildings The Exchange Buildings Graham Road/Church Street
Photos: Author

THE EXCHANGE

THE EXCHANGE

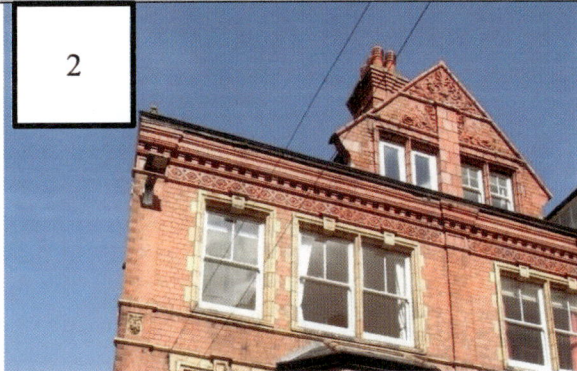

[3]Foliated decoration Terracotta slabs

[4]Buff Terracotta Name Plate

[5]Shoulder joint construction

Fig 63 The 1905 Memorial and Parish Rooms Barnards Green Road

'1905 Memorial and Parish Rooms E Baldwin clay tiled pitched roof/dormer windows and central cupola.(The cupola being a typical Edwardian feature) Elevations in rusticated Cradley stone with buttresses. Gothic style pointed leaded Windows. Front elevation with Gothic style porch in Cradley stone. Arched carved doorway facing the Street. 1905 E. Baldwin' (Pevsner, Alan Brooks and Nicolas, 2007)

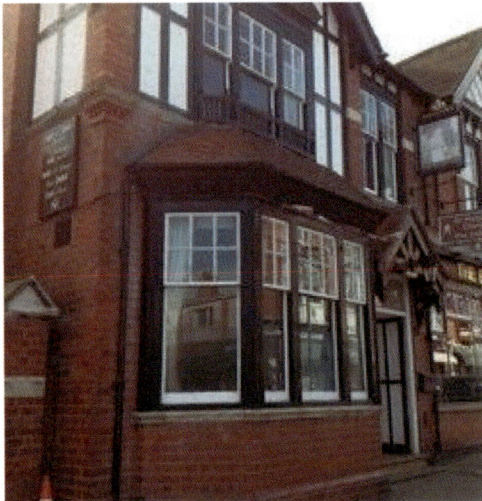

Bakery Inn, Malvern Link   New Gas Tavern (Now Demolished)

Fig 64   Public Houses often took on the Edwardian style and these are two typical examples. Outside the current Great Malvern survey area. Photos: Author

Fig 65 The Old Community Hospital Lansdowne Crescent

Cradley stone, tall chimneys ,distinctive perimeter walling

The Old Community Hospital Lansdowne Crescent was built in 1909-11 by Architect William Henman FRIBA [See 6 .8 in this Guide.] Builders were Braziers. The Benefactor was CW Dyson Perrins of Davenham House who saw the need for a larger premises than the Hospital at Hospital Bank.

Henman specialised in Hospital designs and was Architect for Birmingham Gen Hospital and The Royal Victoria in Belfast.

This design in Malvern almost echoes Lutyens perhaps Henman being influenced by the Arts and Crafts movement. It has fine Art Nouveau detailing including tiles inside.

This building is redundant and thought to be converted into residential or a Care Home [2015.] However it is also under threat of demolition 2015.

The imposing view of rear elevation from the Tennis Club and Albert Road North

78 Graham Road [1/2] is a Typical Edwardian villa built as a pair with number 76. Tiled roof with dormer featuring sunburst design from the Arts & crafts aesthetic movement. Cradley stone rusticated elevations.

Charlfont House 1905 ChristChurch Road [3]. Two storeys, hipped tiled roof on bracketed eaves. Two storey canted central bay with projecting eave detail and dormer window. Original casement mullion windows. Elevations/ upper storey roughcast and half timbering to bay/lower storey brick and stone. *Charlfont House by Marcus O.Type 1905, brick, roughcast and half timbering with hipped roof* (Pevsner, Alan Brooks and Nicolas, 2007).

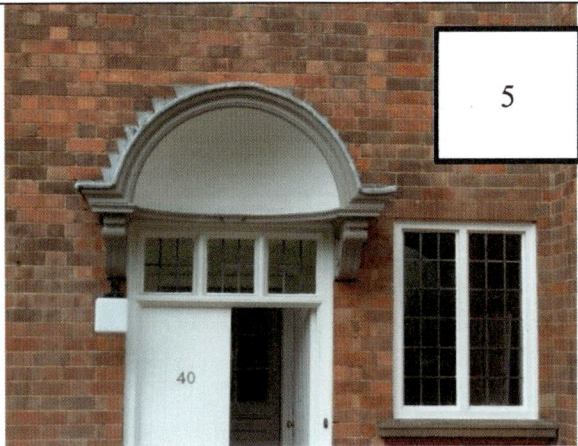

40 Hornyold Rd [4 &5] Two Typical Edwardian Style Villas with typical Edwardian detailing; clay tile roof, brick elevations, Door hood, recessed front door, Edwardian windows. See also 19,Blackmore Road [6&7] All typical Edwardian styling.

Blackmore Road

St Andrews Road [8]A plainer style villa;mix of materials / roughcast and brick and cast iron railings[9]

25 (Broad Meadow) & 27 St Andrews Road are not on 1885 1st Edition Map so built after this date.This is an unusual Edwardian house [10 &11] with Two 'Dutch' style, double height brick end gable bays incorporating four large 1/1 panes large sash windows. No 27 has an internal Art Nouveau glass door and mosaic tiled hallway. To the frontage of both properties there is an ornate cast iron fence typical of the 'Arts & Crafts aesthetic movement' with sun flower designs on a low brick wall .The same fence design divides the two front gardens. More ornate railings can be found nearby in Manby Road [12]

More Ornate Railings in Manby Road.

Railings in Manby Road

In 1885 on the 1st Edition Ordnance map the area below Christ Church in Avenue Road Christchurch Road Malvern did not exist so buildings appear between 1885-1905. Some of these must have been built in the Edwardian period. [1901-1914]

Fig 67 Edwardian buildings around Avenue Road and Christ Church Photos :Author

| 1 | 32 Avenue Road | 2 |

32 Avenue Road Is a Plainer villa style, [1]mix of materials and cast iron gate,[2] sunflower design of which there are a few the same in Malvern and they maybe a signature of the designer/ builder. 1 & 2] Also nearby in Christchurch Road [3 & 4] a Semi-detached and a Terrace .Queen Anne style referencing seen at 38 Avenue road[5] with its wonderful sloping low slung roof[5]

Semi Detached Terracing by Speculative Builders in Christ Church Road

Christchurch Road [3/4] Both terraces have original Edwardian features, half timbering to gables, typical complex patterns of glazing bars to windows.

38 Avenue Road.
Queen Anne Style with a rare Motor House

Motor Houses

As mentioned in Historical Note/Context [9.1] early cars were made in Malvern and with them came the Motor House. Malvern has many but a fine example is a Pre 1914 Motor House, although heavily altered and reclad it is still a rare early survivor (The Victorian Society, 2010)

'This is quite a find. It is probably a pre 1914 motor house and is I suspect a rare survival of an early prefabricated timber motor house. What gives it away is the high roof pitch and the elaborate treatment of the gable. We found very few examples of these during our project so this is an interesting discovery. It has been extensively altered in recent years with new doors and has been reclad.' (Minnis, 23rd June 2014)

Motor House at 38 Avenue Road
(Minnis, 23rd June 2014)

Fig 68   1920s 30s House Parts
Buildings from Malvern Source: Author

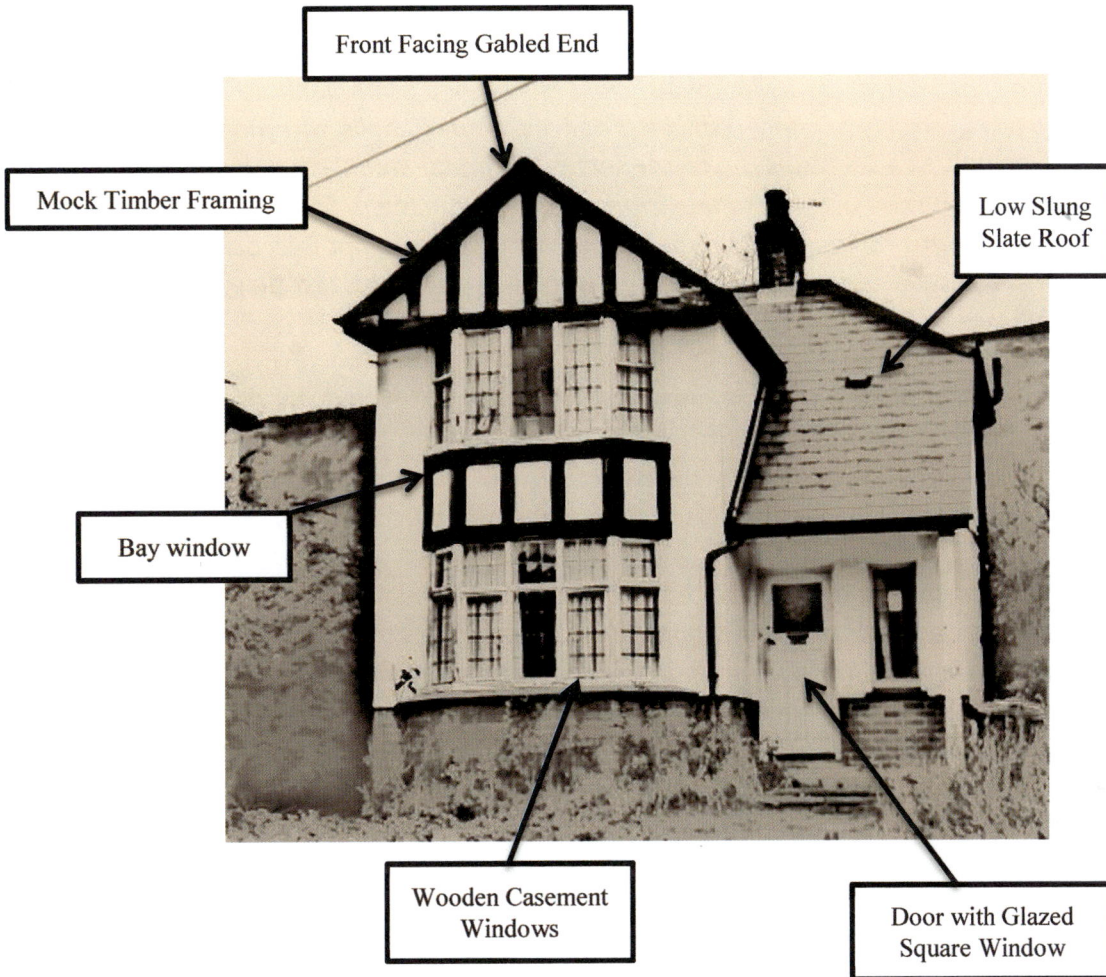

Front Facing Gabled End

Mock Timber Framing

Low Slung Slate Roof

Bay window

Wooden Casement Windows

Door with Glazed Square Window

Except for a few buildings less and less building was being executed in Malvern since the decline of the water cure, and "by the 1920s Malvern was rather an empty town" (Moody, 1953) However by the late 1920s a new festival was born that put Malvern on the map once more. The Malvern Festival founded by Sir Barry Jackson of the Birmingham Repertory Theatre transformed the old Assembly Rooms and Winter Gardens, Grange Road in 1928 – 9. They were purchased by the Council in 1927 under the chairmanship of Dr H.W.Jacob. *The two-week 1929 Festival was entirely the work of playwright Bernard Shaw and by 1930 Sir Edward Elgar, composer, was to have a special place in the Festival that also involved the novel attraction of a Film Festival. By 1933 it was firmly established as an annual event. "The festival was a total social experience: concerts, dances, dinners, balls, afternoon parties, weekend parties….Special trains ran to connect with London and Birmingham" (Covins, 1981)and many famous actors and musicians stayed in the town. Sadly the festival ended on 2nd of September 1939 due to the outbreak of WW2. An attempt was made to revive it and one more Festival was held in 1949 for which Shaw wrote his last play."* (Smith, 1964)

Malvern did not see the same ribbon development or interwar estates that the rest of the country was experiencing at this time apart from a few small ones around Pickersleigh and Hayslan Fields and a strip of development by the railway line in St Andrews Road. Some of the Malvern shopfronts had fashionable 1930s and Art Deco makeovers.

In the rest of the country restrictions introduced in the First World War continued to some degree. Many landlords sold their pre-war properties at cheap prices to sitting tenants. The whole of the middle classes could now own their own home The 1920s saw subsidies to industries by the government to encourage builders of private housing. The Wall Street Crash of 1929 impacted around the globe sending economies into further depression. However there were improved health services, a drop-in death rates and infant mortality, but at the same time there was a reduced birth rate. With fewer children there was more money. The real boom came in the mid-1930s as interest rates fell and lower income families could be considered for a loan. This lasted until the rearmament programme began to push costs up (Lawrence, 2009)

Characteristic layouts used on interwar estates, for example at Welwyn Garden City in 1920 can be recognised on maps, and these can be seen in Malvern on the 1920s Ordnance Survey maps on a small scale. This layout being a forerunner to 'the cul-de-sac 'that is seen up and down Britain today.

 Four million homes were built between the two World Wars, many surrounding the cities in styles that echoed the past. A small number of 'the international style' later named Art Deco followed simple clean line designs much like their counterparts, ship building ,notably the Ocean Liners. Most of these Art Deco buildings were individually designed.

After WW1 the cost of materials and labour increased sharply at the same time that demand shot up for housing. The Government made local authorities provide low cost housing starting a social housing programme that continued through most of the C20 Most of the suburban style housing was similar to the Edwardian period initially for the upper end of the market but by the end of the 1930s there was a boom in less expensive and small houses costing as little as £300. The styles can be described as follows: Mock Tudor/Victorian Edwardian Styles/Art and Crafts 'garden suburbs'/Neo-Georgian/Modern Styles/Modernist or Ultramodern/Art Deco and Low level living. The popularity of the bungalow soared in the 1930s as land was cheap the single-storey bungalow, especially along the coast, became popular. Some experimental building used prefabricated materials, timber frames clad in materials like asbestos, wire coated in render or wooden planks. Four or five storey apartments were erected in cities especially London, those built in the 1920s and 30s have become iconic symbols of the age. Architect Harry Wilson designed the Burton Stores and BC Donaldson Woolworths. Many stores had distinctive faience and art deco frontages. The 400th branch of Woolworths opened at Southport Lancashire in 1930. As the 1930s wore on, Woolworths went slightly Art Deco, cinematic and streamlined. The Neo Georgian Post offices of the 1930s were always more tailor-made than Neo-Georgian council housing (Robert Hradsky, 2010)

Mostly built in red brick, plain red brick with some darker brown varieties, some with pressed patterns in the surface, the most popular types of bonding were Flemish. During this period cavity walls changed little. Mortars gradually became cement-based rather than lime-based because the faster setting mortar meant faster construction. Solid floors began to appear with the use of engineering bricks for damp course membranes rather than slate. Dividing walls were still made from brick although these were now cheaper, by using common bricks like Flettons, as they would be plastered and not visible. Sometimes the new wonder material, the breezeblock (made from Coke breeze, small cinders and dust from furnaces, gasworks and smelters mixed with cement and sand), were used. Machine made clay tiles, Roman tiles, Pantiles, and diamond shaped Asbestos Tiles were used for roof coverings. A style of Round bays/Bow windows, often covered in machine made tiles. Prefabricated materials like asbestos/wire coated render/wooden planks and the use of glazed faience were common. Wooden casement windows were still being used, and were typically painted cream contrasting with frames painted a darker colour such as mid-green or chocolate brown. Also common; bull's-eye windows. Many of the windows were decorated with leaded lights and stained glass. Advances were made in technology for example 'Hopes Metal Casement Windows/Modern Sun Trap Windows' were mass produced by Crittall Ltd of Braintree Essex 1934 and fitted to 'moderne' houses. They also made windows with latticework leading and this combined with half timbering helped to create the 'mock Tudor' look. Metal framed windows gave a modernistic look and were incorporated into many semi-detached houses. There were usually long vertical glazed panels either side of the door and the whole ensemble was commonly placed in a large, round arched, open porch and this, along with the timbered gable and bay window, forms one of the most recognisable stylistic components of a privately built thirties house.

Either red brick/ glazed faience/rough cast harling to elevations were used. Machine made clay tiles or diamond shaped asbestos tiles also popular. Crittall windows or wooden casements/coloured leaded lights on higher class buildings.

Mostly unknown except local architect Troyte Griffth built some notable houses outside this Guides Survey area for individual clients. For example 'The Orchard' Peachfield Road 1931, 'Withybrook Bungalow' King Edwards Road 1938, and others in Colwall, 'Beacons Lea' Brockhill Road in 1924, the latter mentioned by Alan Brooks in the updated Pevsner as 'pink rendered' (Hardie, 2012) In the Survey area are:- F.C.R.Palmers Nat West Bank in Church Street 1930-1, J.R.Armstrong of Bourneville Village Trust 1937-8 for The Friends Meeting House on Orchard Road, E.E.C.Bewley on alterations and additions to Imperial Hotel now Malvern St James School 1932-4 and A.V.Rowe 1927 – 8, Malvern Hills College, Albert Road North built as a School of Art. (Pevsner, Alan Brooks and Nicolas, 2007) and Stanley Griffiths for the Methodist Chapel again outside this survey in Somers Park Road where there are also some domestic 1930s houses.

Methodist Chapel Somers Park Road although not in the Survey has been included as a building of note for the 1930s. Built 1935 Architect Stanley Griffiths of Stourbridge (Dixon, 2011)

1930s House on Somers Park Road with all 30s details intact 2014. Crittall leaded windows, recessed porch doorway with 30s arch

Fig 69 1930s Somers Park Road Photos: Author

Fig 70 Commercial 1930s Buildings of Note Photos: Author

24, Church St the 'Art Deco' Woolworths in house design. [1,2,3,4]
Current building is one of only two Art Deco buildings in Great Malvern, the 1930s Woolworths 'in house' design. Horribly defaced with plastic paint [4] and sometime after 1970s [1] when its glazed faïence exterior could still be seen.

Left [1].Woolworths in the 1970s with the 1930s glazed ceramic faience clearly on view. Above [2.] 2010 when Woolworth branches closed forever.

Left [3.]photo shows the buildings today now an Iceland Store. Above [4.] a close up of the paint covering the faience Art Deco design.

Fig 71 Malvern Art Deco Shopfronts Photos: Author

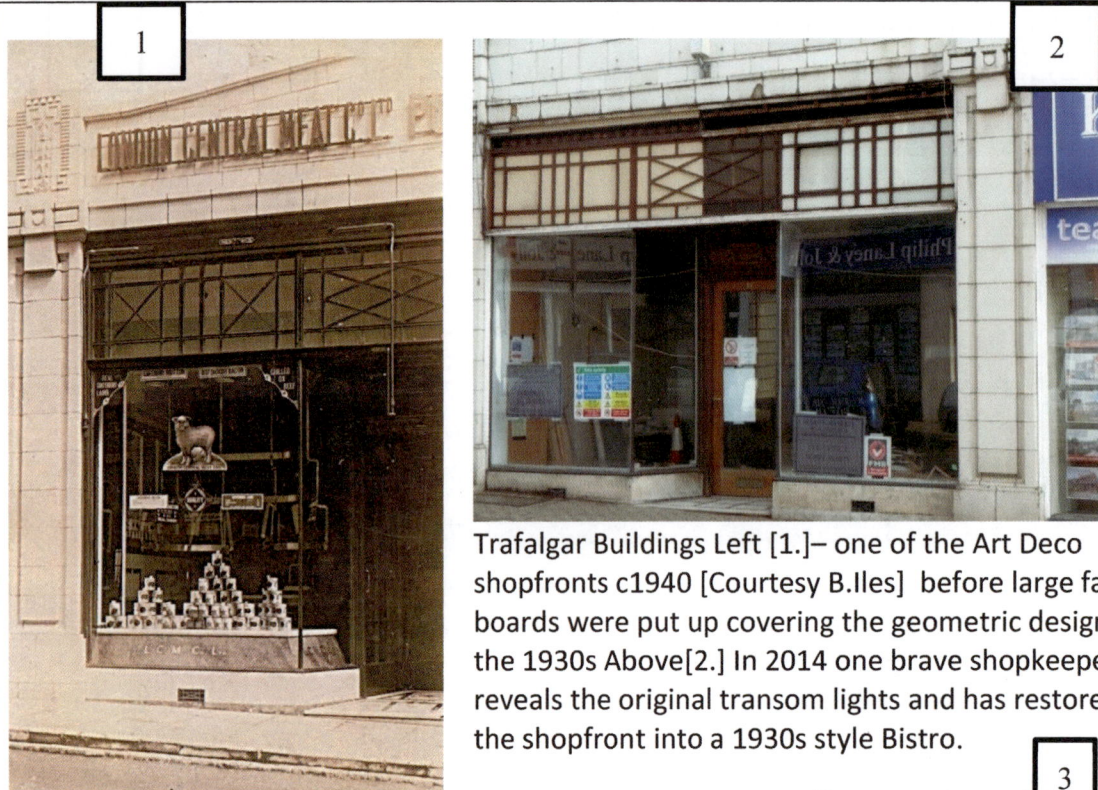

Trafalgar Buildings Left [1.]– one of the Art Deco shopfronts c1940 [Courtesy B.Iles] before large fascia boards were put up covering the geometric design of the 1930s Above[2.] In 2014 one brave shopkeeper reveals the original transom lights and has restored the shopfront into a 1930s style Bistro.

Montage photo of all shop fronts [3]c1960 before alterations [Courtesy B.Iles]

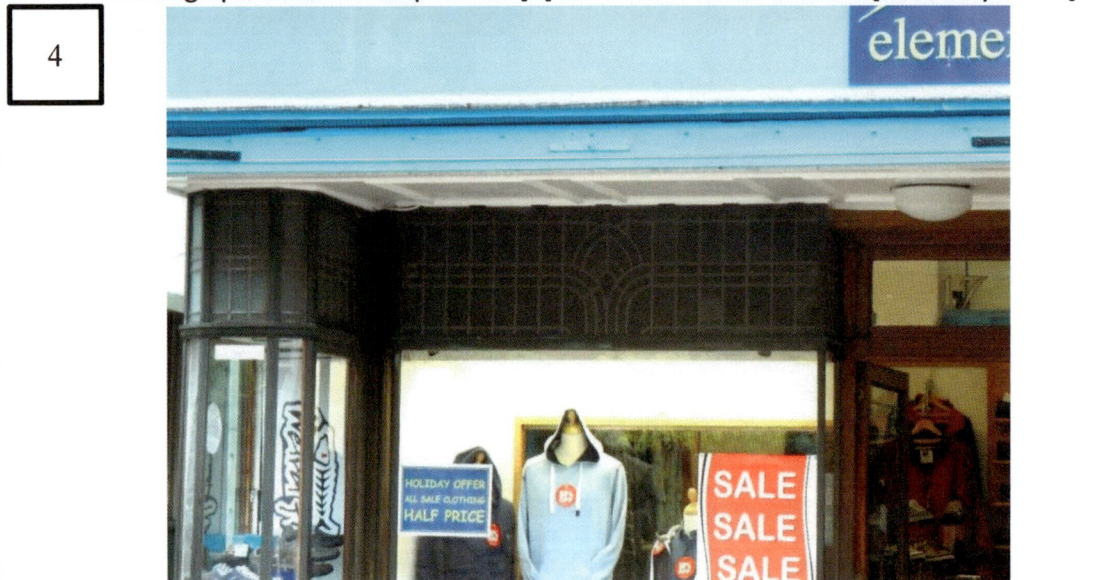

'Elements' shopfront in Church Street has a 1930s transom with leaded lights

Art Deco shop front and Arcade **GDII** Listed building on Belle Vue Terrace
This is a rare survivor of 1930s[5] with brass shop windows that form part of a small Arcade

Fig 72 1930s Neo Georgian

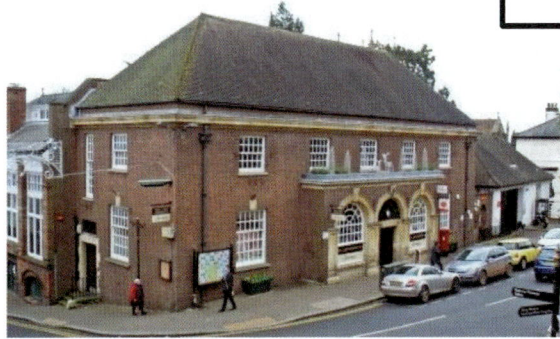

Left [1] is a Neo Georgian Shop now the Tourist Information Centre . Above [2] The 1930s tailor-made Neo-Georgian Post Office [in house design.] Below [3]. The former Art College *by A.V.Rowe 1927 – 8* Albert Road North (Pevsner, Alan Brooks and Nicolas, 2007) Now South Worcestershire College

Fig 73 1920s/30s Pavilions Photos: Author

1920s/30s Pavilions seen at the Tennis Club [1] and Bowling Club [2] Leisure pursuits were popular in the 1930s. The Tennis Club relocated to their current site during this time and the pavilion reflects this.[1] The Bowling Club also has a 1920s/30s Pavilion beside Priory Park. [2] Probably added when the Council gained The Assembly Rooms for the Festival

[3] The 'Friends Meeting House' located on Orchard Road 1937-8 J.R.Armstrong of Bourneville Village Trust designed the building. Pale brick with big hipped pantiled roof coming forward over projecting porch. Venetian type window South end (Pevsner, Alan Brooks and Nicolas, 2007)

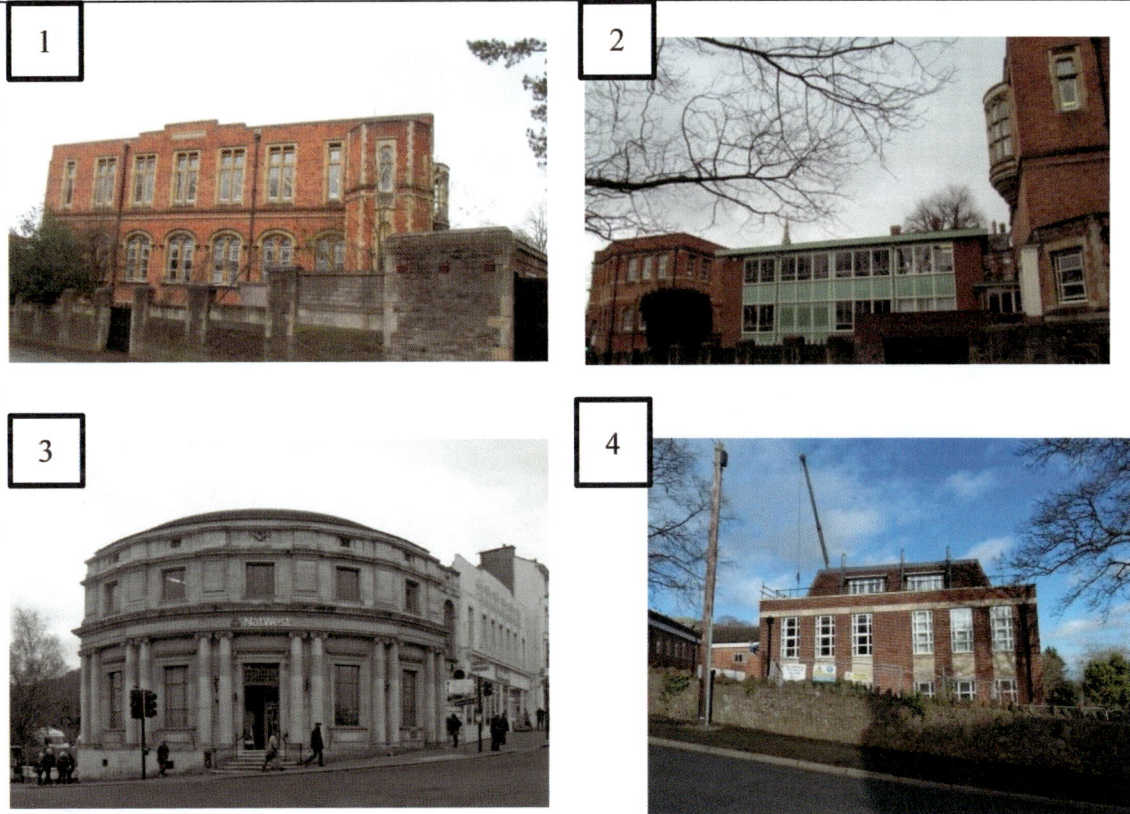

Above the additions to the now[1.] Malvern St James School *1932 – 4 by E E.C.Bewley added large two storey brick wing at the rear of the former hotel, and the [2.]* 1929 – 30 classroom block on the site of Hotels Brine Baths (Pevsner, Alan Brooks and Nicolas, 2007) Also [3] Nat West Bank on corner of Church Street on site of older 1885 building Athol House & Truro House .Curved stone faced , with original Crittal windows   *1930-31 by F.C.R.Palmer* (Pevsner, Alan Brooks and Nicolas, 2007) *[4.]* The Preston Science Block Malvern College .

The Assembly rooms, now Malvern Theatres underwent alterations during this time as previously mentioned but further alterations were made in the 1980s so little of the 1930s style remains

Fig 75 1930s.Bungalows of note and typical of 1930s style Photos: Author

Housing

Only those 1930s houses and bungalows that still maintain some or all original details are shown as examples in this section. There are only a few as this period in Architecture seems prone to many alterations and replacement windows unlike the previous eras. Perhaps the quality of timber for windows was inferior and Crittall windows ill-fitting or perhaps owners just did not like the architectural detailing and the use of Asbestos.

35 Clarence Road[1]

1920/30s Stanley Road[2]

These two bungalows [1 and 2] still retain their Asbestos diamond roof coverings and casement windows. Stanley Road is outside the Guide Survey. The following are more elaborate with their detailing and have timber framing and curved recessed porches/doorways. The one in St Andrews Rd has an integral garage that looks original.

71 Peachfield Road (Orchard Cottage) above.[3]
Left St Andrews Road with possibly integral garage

Fig 76 1930s Small detached houses Photos: Author

Typical of the Suburban style these are detached and not semi-detached so in the 30s would have been seen as more superior. Some have round arched, open porches and this, along with the timbered gable [1] creates the mock Tudor look. The two storey bay window, forms one of the most recognisable stylistic components of a privately built thirties house.

60 St Andrews Rd[1]with all original 30s details intact

64 St Andrews Rd[2] This one has some alterations but is a good example

163 Newtown Road [3]
Low slung tiled roof incorporating a tiled arched recessed porch/ doorway. Timber framing and roughcast elevations. Six leaded light window to front elevation

Fig 77   Post WW2 House Parts
Buildings from Malvern Source: Author

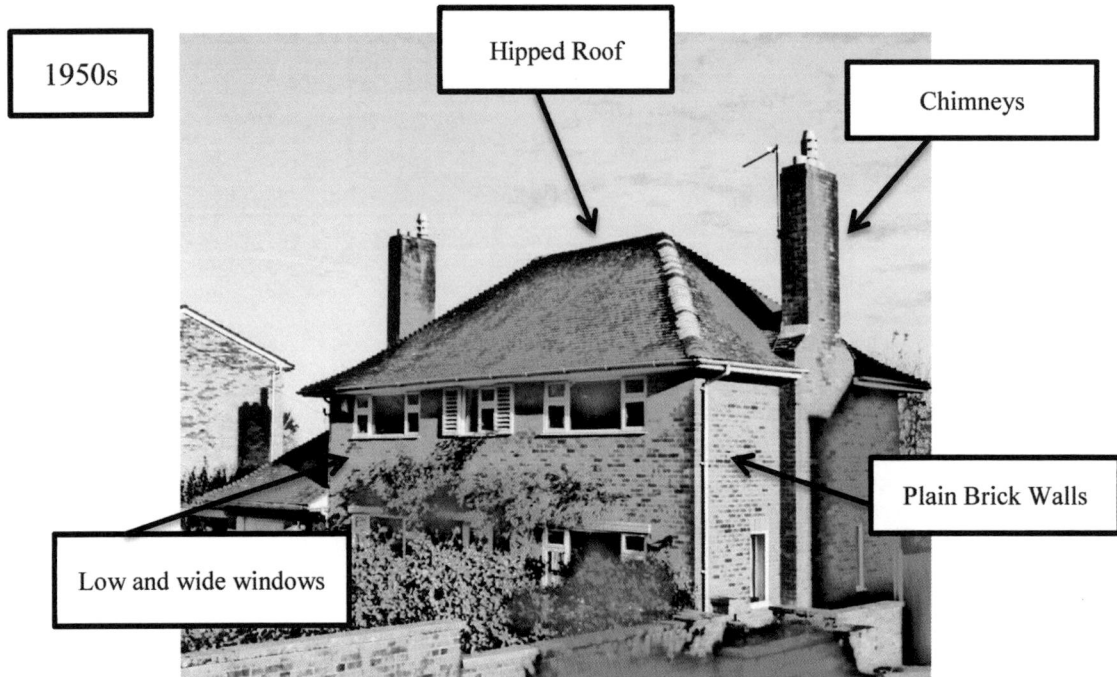

1950s

Hipped Roof

Chimneys

Plain Brick Walls

Low and wide windows

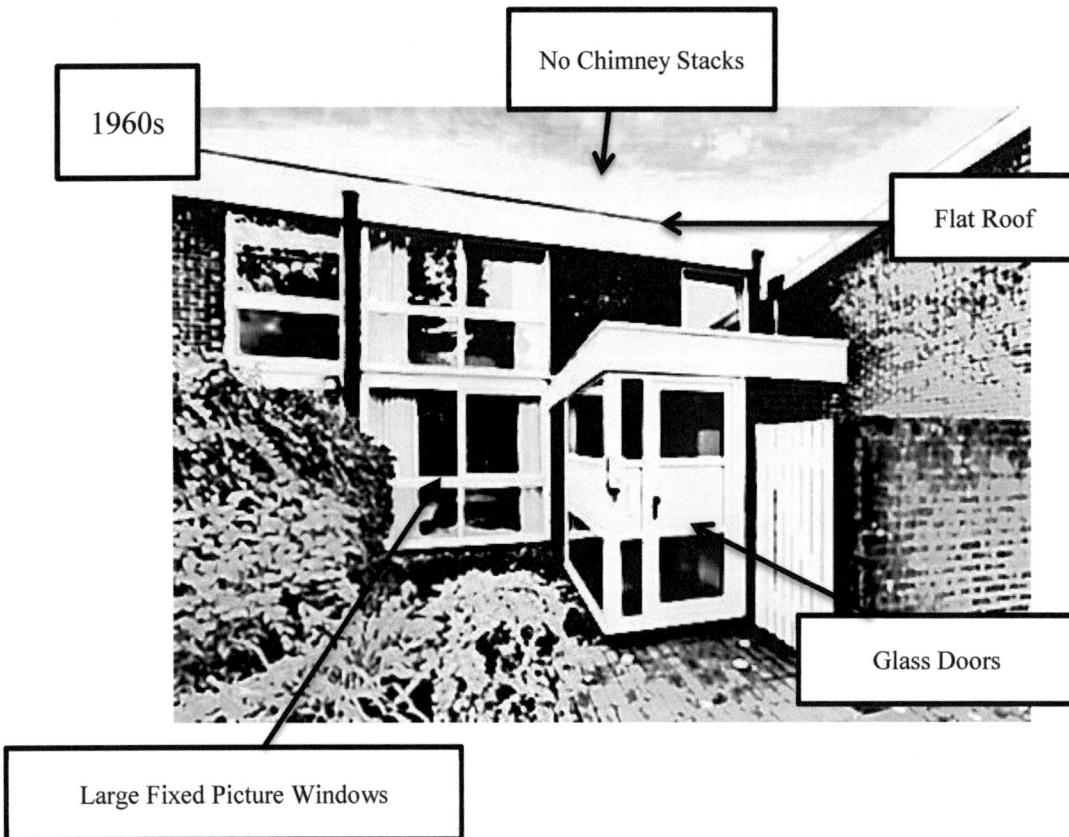

No Chimney Stacks

1960s

Flat Roof

Glass Doors

Large Fixed Picture Windows

The outbreak of the Second World War effectively put a stop to house building for a second time. As the war drew to a close Britain faced its worst housing shortage of the twentieth century. Thousands of houses across the country had been lost by heavy bombing and many more were badly damaged. It was estimated that 750,000 new homes were required in England and Wales in 1945 to provide all families with accommodation.

However Malvern was very fortunate and did not suffer much if any bomb damage

The Author Catherine Moody in 1953 said *'Now since the recent war a different phase has begun from which a new Malvern is growing. The arrival of Government Research Establishments and a permanent increase in population, for the first time for many years, has caused an increase in domestic building which has added an outer zone to the town'* (Moody, 1953)

Both T.R.E and R.R.D.E came to Malvern in WW2 an unwelcome surprise for many local residents. Thought to be merely passing the scientists were here to stay and the population grew. Permanent 'glass and concrete' buildings at The Royal Radar Establishment were added in 1955. Large estates at Pickersleigh, Poulbrook and Cockshot Road were built for the Ministry of Supply, on Council land, whilst the Council itself built housing estates in Malvern Link and Sherrards Green. The first Secondary Modern Schools were built, The Chase 1953 and Dysons Perrins in 1959. The Three Counties Agricultural Show began in 1958. In 1960 the town continued its development in the Tourist industry, and the private schools still flourished. (Smith, 1964)

In the 1960s The Spring Lane industrial estate was set up (The Enigma business Park and Retail Park built in the 1990s due to land being sold by the Madresfield Estate.) During the 1960s, 70s and 80s the Malvern Winter Gardens (now Malvern Theatres)was a major regional venue for rock concerts; groups such as The Rolling Stones, T Rex, The Jam, AC/DC, Black Sabbath, Thin Lizzy, The Stranglers. It underwent a major refurbishment in 1995 and became the Malvern Festival Theatre Trust. In 1997 the Malvern Theatres opened once more following a 5.2 million pound award from the National Lottery

Viewed from the Malvern Hills on North Hill can be seen several developments in the sprawl of North Malvern. Late 1940s social housing of Jamaica Road and the 1970s private housing estate of Oak Road

11.2 The Style 1950s

Pre-Fabs were built as demand for new housing and as 'Homes For Heroes' .The Height of these houses was generally lower than pre-war, they were of simplified design and economic. In the 1951 Festival of Britain a new council estate was used as the site for new architecture by leading designers. Colours were, vibrant and pastel shades were used for interiors. (Hoskins, 1998)This was the age of the beginning of 'Do-it-yourself.' Front elevations were plain-sandy light brown or pale bricks or broken up with areas of render or hanging tiles. There was some influence of American and Scandinavian building, designs that used glass and prefabricated elements for instance. For the middle class large bungalows pierced by a prominent chimney of rough-hewn stone (See Fig 78   [8]) were popular or a chalet style house with a steep pitched roof. A duty to make housing provision for older people meant there was purpose built elderly housing (See Fig 78 [7] Isabelle Harrison)

11.3 Materials 1950s

Pre-Fabs were built to meet the shortage and bring the cost of housing down. A new form of construction was pioneered, commonly called 'PRC' (Pre-cast Reinforced Concrete). These houses were quick to assemble and required less skilled labour than traditional build. There were proprietary brands developed and marketed by different builders, steel frames covered in Asbestos sheets, or pebbledash/ vertical concrete slabs. Pre Fabs came in various kinds and styles such as the Airey, Cornish, Wates, Unity Reema, Tarran, Woolaway and Parkinson types. Other Houses of the period had plain brick walls, shallow pitch gable roofs, low and wide metal framed windows with plain doorways with a flat slab as a porch. Larger houses or bungalows used a mix of materials.

11.4 Materials used in Malvern in relation to style. 1950s

Airey Homes and Cornish Units were built in Malvern and were largely made from concrete panels reinforced with steel then bolted together or constructed with a steel frame. Private Housing and Small Estates had plain brick walls, shallow pitch gable roofs with low and wide metal framed windows with plain doorways with a flat slab as a porch. Larger houses or bungalows used a mix of materials. The Malvern Cornish units are set to be be demolished in 2015.

11.5 Malvern architects1950s

Architects for the Ministry of Supply, on Council land. The Council itself built Housing Estates in Malvern Link and Sherrards Green and used in house Architects.

Fig 78   1945-60 Malvern Examples All Photos: Author

Cornish Units[1] soon to be demolished. (above) Airey Homes [2]safe at the moment, the photograph (right) has been unaltered from when it was built.

Airey Homes **[2]**Regency Road Malvern

[3]Police Station Victoria Road built in the 50s opened early 60s

16 Victoria Road-Typical 50s villa style[4] beside the Police station

42 Albert Road North. These were built for the Police families. This example retains all 50s details. [5]

42 Albert Road North 50s Gate[6]

Isabelle Harrison Gardens Worcester Road Malvern Link. Homes for the Elderly in the 1950s [7] Outside Survey Area for Guide but worth noting. Still in use as Homes for Elderly.

In Victoria Road an example of a house with prominent chimney of rough-hewn stone[8]

11.7 The Style 60s and 70s

It was high rise living 'streets in the air' mostly in the cities to house the masses a good example is the 'Park Hill Estate' in Sheffield. Brutalist Architect was vogue and influential. Cast Concrete materials were used for example at The South Bank Centre and the Birmingham Central library. For House Styles in the 1960s- blockwork was almost universal in inner leaf. Timber casement windows and centre pivot windows became popular. Houses had flat roofs or even shallow pitched roofs. Individually Architect designed modernist houses were built for the wealthy incorporating open plan designs.

11.8 Materials 60s and 70s

Block and steel, cavity wall construction with brickwork tied with galvanised steels twist or wire. Mortar was cement based. Concrete interlocking roof tiles were common or flat roofs covered in bitumen felt or copper. Guttering was now plastic. Plasterboard used instead of lath and plaster. Large timber casements or fixed picture windows were the style.

11.9 Materials used in Malvern in relation to style. 60s and 70s

Block and steel, cavity wall construction with brickwork tied with galvanised steels twist or wire. Mortar was cement based. Concrete interlocking roof tiles were common or flat roofs covered in bitumen felt or copper. Guttering was now plastic. Plasterboard used instead of lath and plaster. Large timber casements or fixed picture windows were the style.

Fig 79 Examples of 1960s and 70s in Malvern   Photos :Author

Terrace of 1960s houses Graham Road (above[1])
Semi-detached housing 60s style Graham Road (Right)[2]Typical examples of shallow roof and flat roof. Large windows.

Hatfield House.Imperial Road *[3] "Imperial Road Brick/concrete construction with a mix of metal and timber windows set inside the large curtain wall panels A middle school house 1963-4 by T.H.B Burrough workmanlike concrete framing with brick and curtain wall infill, and many polygonal projections and recessions (resembling beehives) Butterfly-plan entrance with central concrete porch; small lobby with spiral concrete staircase" (Alan Brooks, 2007)*

Smaller blocks of Flats (above) using mix of materials[4]

Smaller block with a Mansard roof[5]

Hardwicke House in Abbey Road [6] on the site of the demolished Hardwicke House, a Gothic mansion built for Dr. Marsden and Hydropathy.(See Section 6.] This is Malverns bit of Brutalist Architecture. Photo Below shows typical balconies and fenestration looking out of place in Malvern but having good views [7]over the Severn Plain for the occupants

Community buildings of the 1960s (left [8]) are the Community Centre, now Malvern Cube. It is still used as Community/Youth Centre on Albert Road North. Low rise, flat bitumen roofs. Pale bricks.

The Dome 1970s below is a now GDII Listed [9] A rare Concrete structure with copper roof.

Typical [10] bungalow of the 1970s

The Dome

11.11 The Style 80s and 1990s

The style in the 1980s and 90s was vaguely Edwardian looking. Terraced houses built by Barretts or the Laing 'Pimlico' [one bedroom apartments]. Old warehouses were converted for Yuppies (Young and upwardly mobile) and Dinkys (Double income no kids yet) New build tended to be bland but there was a property boom. As soon as you had bought a current model there was a better and bigger one on the market. Traditional appearance of dormer windows, hipped roofs, gable ends exposed timbers and overlapping first floors with an absent of a chimney, the dead giveaway to dating, concrete pantiles, Georgian lookalike windows, fake leaded lights, lever door handles, resin coated woodwork, clapboarding and rendering. All have been minimalized to use the thinnest possible walls and smallest amounts of building materials. (Martin Pawley, 1992)

11.12 Materials

Cavity wall construction was virtually universal with brick, stone or artificial stone in the outer leaf and aerated blocks in the inner leaf. The inner lead could be 130mm in order to achieve the appropriate U value (0.6 in 1985). Plastic windows were now available but most developers used standard metric timber windows (usually of casement design and often with no top lights). Roof coverings were mostly of concrete interlocking tiles, often similar in profile to pantiles or double romans, sometimes with non-traditional profiles (e.g. Redland Delta).

11.13 Materials used in Malvern in relation to style.

In Malvern materials used were Cavity walls with a brick or render skin. Concrete roof coverings and Plastic or Aluminium windows.

The Splash Indoor Swimming Pool was built in 1989,[2] The Retail Park was built in the 1990s [1]with Superstores Somerfield then Morrison's[3]. *1999*

'Some 10,000m2 of hillside was excavated and re-laid in a massive cut and fill operation to create a level platform for the two storey supermarket and car parking. The value of construction works was £9.4m and timber crib retaining walls up to 8.5m high were required' (http://hurstpm.net/36-supermarkets, n.d.)

Stores like Waitrose [4] added to the already nearby 1980s Somerfield [5] in the centre of town. The Malvern Theatres underwent major refurbishments and alterations from the Heritage Lottery in 1997[6]

Fig 80 Examples of 1980s-2000 in Malvern Photos: Author

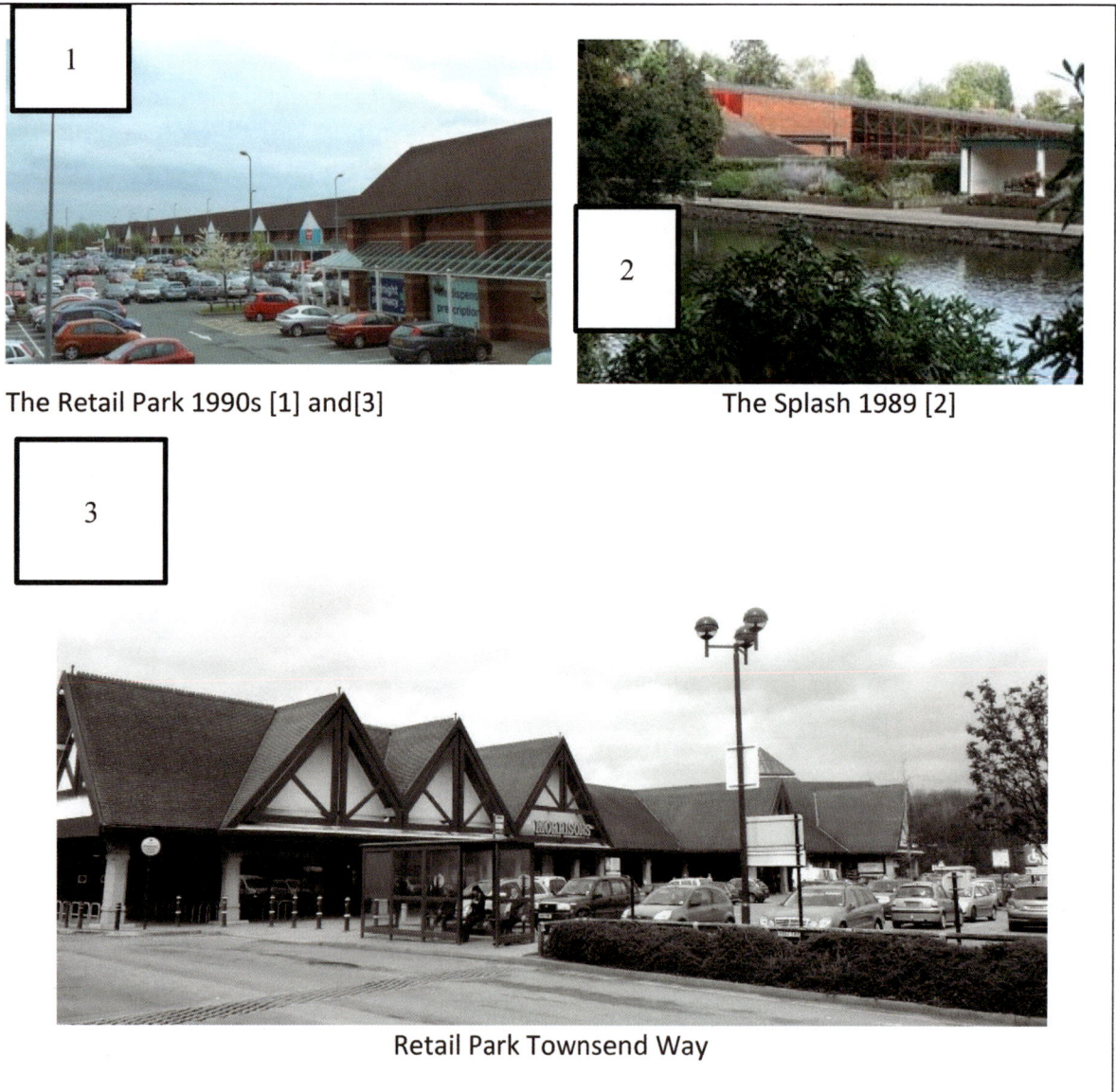

The Retail Park 1990s [1] and[3]

The Splash 1989 [2]

Retail Park Townsend Way

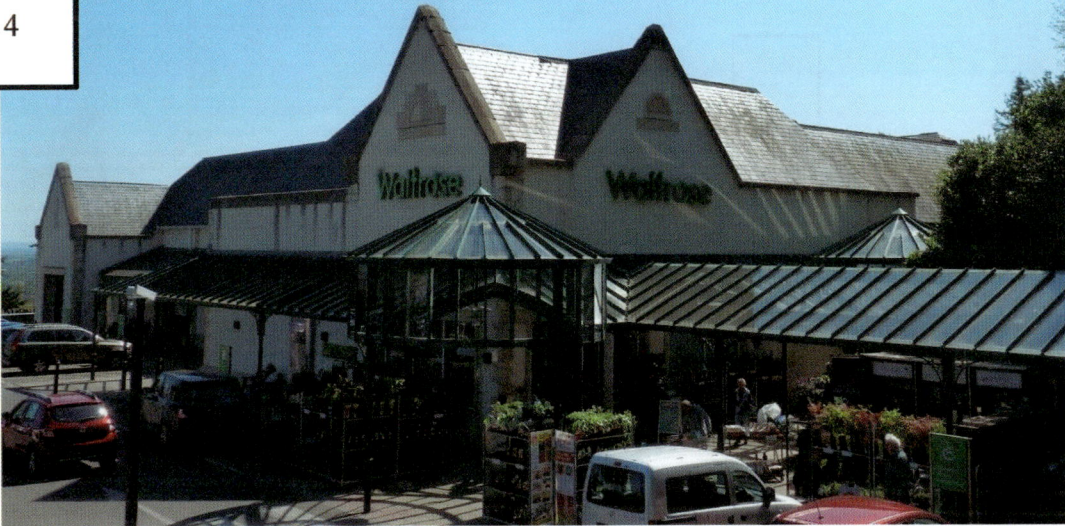

Waitrose built on the market site and carpark 1999 [4]

Today this building is a Wilkinsons Store 2014 [5]

"Built as the International in the 1980s promising an indoor bakery, fresh fish counter, butchery and even a creche. All soon went. Became Somerfields[5] and briefly a Co-op. An alley way, Church Walk, was created to connect the supermarket to the main shopping street, Church Street, by removing one shop. This walkway continues past the supermarket to Edith Walk"

Source: http://www.geograph.org.uk/ http://www.geograph.org.uk/photo/2376843, Credit: Bob Embleton 2011

Malvern Theatres

With Heritage Lottery in 1997 alterations were made to Malvern Theatres[6]
The centre pedimental doorway and raised centre tower are all that remain of the original
Winter Gardens. In this photo [6] the cupola on the roof of the original C19 theatre can be
seen. [7]

Malvern—Assembly Rooms in Foreground.

Malvern Assembly Rooms Source: Malvern Library Archive Directories

Fig 81   C21 House Parts
Buildings from Malvern Source: Author

Landmark Modernist Style

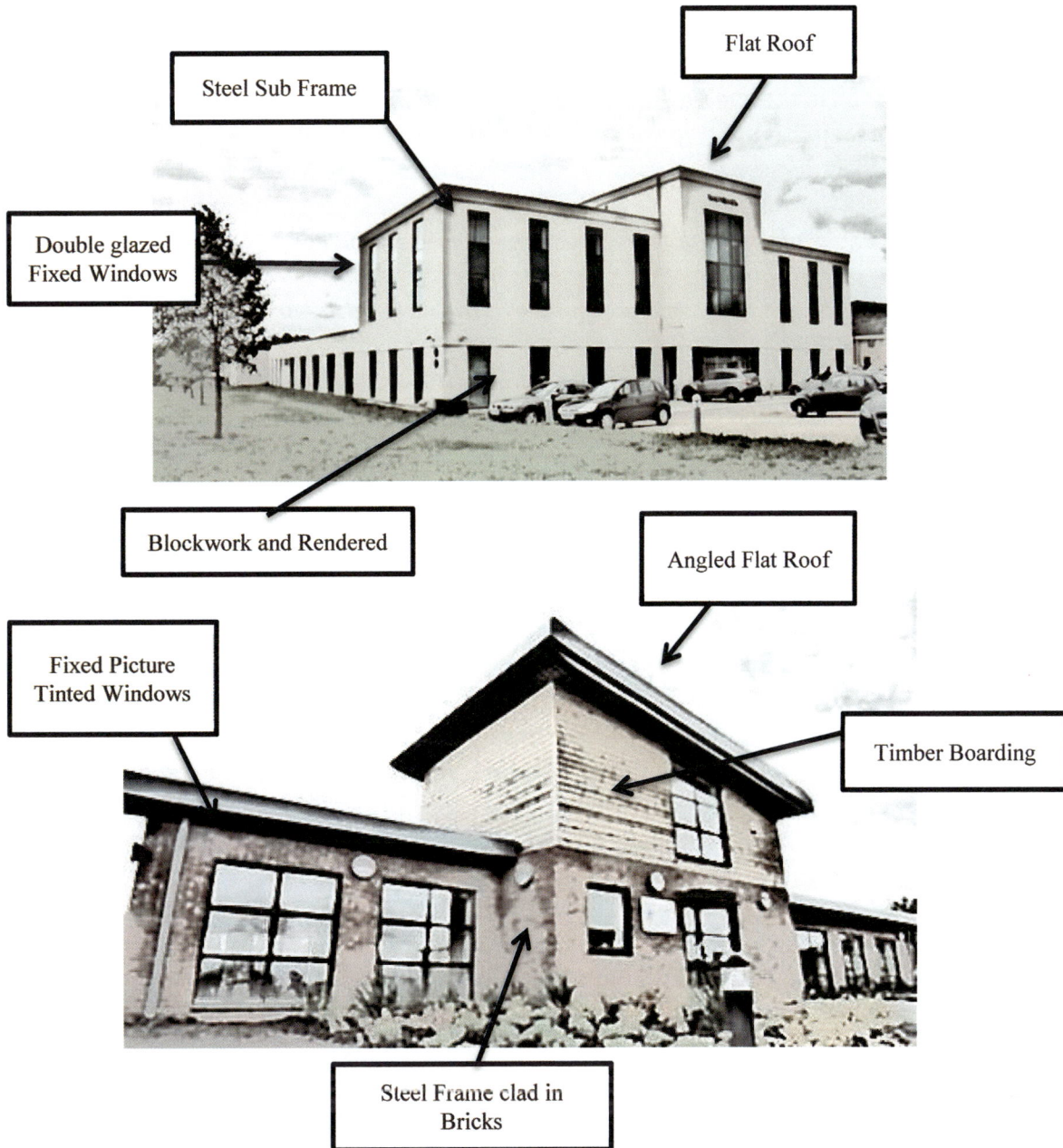

Steel Sub Frame

Flat Roof

Double glazed
Fixed Windows

Blockwork and Rendered

Angled Flat Roof

Fixed Picture
Tinted Windows

Timber Boarding

Steel Frame clad in
Bricks

With the arrival of the new millennium Britains real estate and land was at premium value. Most people owned or aspired to own their own homes. Mortgages were made readily available with the population being able to take out loans, often far exceeding their incomes.

"In 30 years to 2011 house prices have increased by 119%. In 1971 the average house in today's money cost 63,000 K in 2013 it is 169,000 K" (Conservation Bulletin, 2014)

In 2007/8 the bubble burst and there was a financial crash which meant much negative equity on property. In 2014 we have supposedly come out of this recession but property prices are still way above the average income and unaffordable for many, especially in the south and London. There is a shortage of houses for the ever increasing rise in population and there is very little Council owned estates. There has been some attempt to reuse existing housing stock during the last 20 years by companies such as Urban Splash *"with advice from English Heritage urban Splash revitalised Sheffield City Council's grade II*Park Hill housing scheme in a way that preserves historic significance of its reinforced concrete frame while allowing substantial changes to the internal layout and active infill panels"* (Conservation Bulletin, 2014).
However in the C21 there has been an increase in modern housing developments and there is a mismatch between demand for housing and the available supply. With this brings threats and opportunities for the historic environment.

In Malvern since 2000 the building developments have been the ex-DEFRA (North site) a large development called Malvern Vale at North Site, developer Persimmon Homes. Up to 490 houses plus a primary school (not built) and community building, as well as providing land for employment use and a playing field. The first residents moved in in 2008. Malverns Local Plan merged with other local authorities. The South Worcestershire Development Plan, SWDP, (http://www.swdevelopmentplan.org/, 2014) The SWDP is a planning blueprint mapping out where development should take place until 2030. The SWDP has allocated other sites in Malvern for housing including a large site at Newland, where 700 houses are planned on green fields at the edge of Malvern , and a large brownfield site on now disused Science Park (buildings to be demolished) at QinetiQ for a further 250 properties

Recently planning permission was granted to build a housing development of 90 homes on the Clerkenwell fields by Festival Housing Ltd with Bridgehouse Property Consultants meaning demolishing the 1950s Cornish units that are past their best but still enjoy open green spaces.

Many of Malverns Victorian Villas and Hotels have been refurbished into luxury apartments and extra housing has often been allowed in the gardens of these, sometimes referred to as 'garden grabbing'. Recently two 'new build' retirement villages have been built, Cartwright Court by McCarthy and Stone and Clarendon Village by Fortis as assisted living for the elderly. Time will tell if Malverns infrastructure will be able to cope. New Sports Halls have been built by the remaining two private schools and there have been new Health Centres, a new Hospital and Fire Station and a makeover for Malvern Link Railway Station.

12.2 The Style

For commercial buildings the C21 is the age of High-Tech Architecture/Landmark Architecture and with this it is possible to build any shape or form from the high-rise Shard Tower to the new Birmingham New Street train station. The Shard in London built in 2012 by London Bridge a Key Skyscraper in England designed by RPBW. At a height of 309.6 metres (1,016 feet) and with a total 72 occupied floors it reaches skyward into a breath taking 15 storey spire, the Shard London Bridge Quarter is set to be the tallest building in Western Europe in London. Other styles and shapes are numerous good examples are 'The Public', the 'New Library' in Birmingham and more recently 2012 for Worcestershire the golden-cladded riverside Hive in Worcester.This was a unique collaboration between the University of Worcester and Worcestershire County Council .The Hive is Europes first fully integrated and jointly run university and local authority library. 2013 saw the opening of 'the new' Birmingham Library, with the fate of the old by Madin still undecided.

For domestic housing there has been a continuation of style used from the 1980s and 90s of the pastiche, mostly tightly packed (filing cabinet designs) square boxes with little design value. More imaginative social housing schemes seem to previal abroad in Belgium, Amsterdam, France and Copenhagen.

12.3 Materials

For large commercial buildings- steel frames clad in metal/aluminium panels/glass/and timber boarding and plastics.

For domestic housing often of a timber framed construction or breezeblock construction is used. Clad in one brick thick walls/rendered, using concrete tiled roofs with UPVC windows, often quickly built with poor quality materials.

12.4 Materials used in Malvern in relation to style.

Malvern's commercial building is largely constructed using steel frames/ block built clad in bricks /timber cladding / or cement rendered with an added square or two of 'Malvern Stone' except that it is not as Malvern stone is no longer allowed to be quarried. The stone used is Forest of Dean. Malvern stone seems to have been chosen as a design narrative/reference when it is no longer available. Other references could be used such as 'gothic' or 'roughcast' (not pebbledash) or relieving arches with decorative infills or none at all. For Malvern's housing developments, mostly redbrick is preferred, 'filing cabinet' designs with little design merit. Above all 'new build' perhaps should reflect Malverns Architectural Heritage from the past. Whatever the style all newly built buildings should be of high quality materials and of good design with care for layout so not to disturb the 'garden city' principles pioneered by Lady Foley and the Mason Family

Fig 82 Two Modern housing schemes Malvern Source: Author

113

Generally it is Developers with their own 'in house' Architects such as McCarthy and Stone and Fortis/ Festival housing and Persimmon Homes. Crystalight Ltd was established in 1996 and owns many of the historic buildings awaiting development, Cloisters View Developments Ltd with Ansam Construction Ltd is another Developer. (Tudor Court, Wells Road) Some independent architectural firms have designed contemporary Malvern houses such as Architect Nick Carroll from Worcester.

The most recent addition to the Malvern skyline has been the Cartwright Court [1]A complex that copies the C19 Aldwyn Tower and Link Tower Italianate style in a rather pastiche way but it is well executed by McCarthy and Stone. Unfortunately the rather bold design for a fire station from the 1980s[4] has been demolished to make way for a more pastiche 'in house' fire station design[3] with added mock 'Malvern stone' panels. Others of note are the contemporary house on Worcester Road [5] that fits well between the C19 gothic and C19 Regency villas but did it really have to have a mock Malvern Stone panel above the portico? Landmark designs include the Sports complexes added by Malvern College[11] and Malvern St James.[12] Other contemporary buildings attempt to pick design references but in a rather fussy way and Malvern Link station[7] mimics a Heritage Victorian style.

Fig 83 Notable C21 Examples Photos: The author

[1] Cartwright Court [2] The rather stark Malvern Spa building on Townsend Way

[3] The 'new' Fire Station Link Common that replaced the unusual triangular design [4]

[5] Contemporary House Worcester Road by Architect Nick Carroll

[6] The new Malvern Hospital that incorporates some mock Malvern Stone facings

[7] Malvern Link station makeover with mock 'Malvern stone' that is Forest Of Dean [8] The 'new' boarding house accommodation at Malvern College [9] housing complex Priory Road and [10] Clarendon Retirement Village on the outskirts in Malvern Link with mock Malvern stone panels

[11] Sports Hall Malvern College and [12] Sports Hall Malvern St James with turf roof. Real C19 Malvern stone curtilage walling already in situ.

13. Street Index Listed Buildings

KEY
Addresses In Bold. See photo in
Guide in the Section if referred to
E.g. 5.6 or 1.8

Priory Road, 52,

Somers Park Road, Ascension Church 8.6

St Anns Road, 1 And 2,

St Anns Road, 26, Charles House,

St Anns Road, 28 Or 36, Upper Hill House,

St Anns Road, 3, Rose Cottage,

St Anns Road, Aldwyn Tower, 5.6

St Anns Road, Kensington Cottage,

St Anns Road, Red Lion Public House,

St Anns Well,

Thirlestane rd, Number 3 And 4, Boarding House,

Thirlestane, Number 6, Boarding House,

Wells Road, 1 And 2, Holyrood House, 4.5

Wells Road, 21 Adelaide House,

Wells Road, 23, South Villa,

Wells Road, Emmanuel Evangelical Church,

Wells Road, Southlands, Ellerslie School

Wells Road, The Tudor Court,6.12

Wells Road, Cobnash 8.5

Worcester Road, 102, The Vaults,

Worcester Road, 12, Was Coburg Baths,

Worcester Road, 2, 6, 8, Barclays Bank,3.6

Worcester Road, 26, Foley House,

Worcester Road, 28 And 30, Town Club,

Worcester Road, 32 And 30, Burford House,3.6

Worcester Road, 34, Bredon Hotel,

Worcester Road, 36, Brankston,

Worcester Road, 38, Ivy Crest, Worcester Road, 40 – 42, Sidney House,

Worcester Road, 44, Montréal House,

Worcester Road, 46 – 48, Oriel Villa,4.5

Worcester Road, 50, Worfield House,

Worcester Road, 52, Elm Bank,

Worcester Road, 54, Aucott House,3.6

Worcester Road, 55 – 58, Sidmouth House,

Worcester Road, 56, Abberley House,

Worcester Road, 60, Sidmouth Cottage,

Worcester Road, 62,

Worcester Road, 64,

Worcester Road, Foley Arms Hotel,

Worcester Road, Holy Trinity Church, Link Top,

Worcester Road, St Anne's Orchard,

Worcester Road, The Unicorn Public House, 1.8

Zetland Road, 5, Laburnum Cottage,

14. Street Index Buildings of Interest

KEY
Addresses In Bold. See photo in Guide in Section referred to. Other numbers not bold after address refer to age/date 1-12. Refer to Guide for Style.
1-Medieval/C17
2.-1714-1790
3. 1790-1837 Classical
4. 1790-1837 Gothick
5.1830-1900 Classical
6.1830-1900 Gothic
7.1890s
8.1870-1914 Arts & Crafts
9.1901-1914 Edwardian
10.1920s/1930s
11.1950s/60s/70s/80s/90s
12.C21 2000-2014

Church Street, 101 – 103, Gt Malvern Hotel 5
Church Street, 17, T I Centre, 10.6
Church Street, Elements 10.6
Church Street, 24, Iceland, 10.6
Church Street, 3 – 7, 5
Church Street, 30, Natwest Bank, 10.6
Church Street, 38, Chartwell House, 5.6
Church Street, 40, Rockcliffe, 6.12
Church Street, 97 – 99, 5
Church Street, Exchange Building, 9.6
Church Street, Gentleman's Club, 6.12
Church Street, Lyttleton School, 1.7, 9
Church Street, Post Office, 10.6
Clarence Road, 12, Mill Side, 3
Clarence Road, 2, 7
Clarence Road, 35, 10.6
Clarence Road, 4, 7
Clarence Road, 6, 7
Cockshot Road, 2, 9
Cockshot Road, 4, 9
College Grove, 1, 8.6
College Grove, 3, (Rear) 8
College Grove, 3, Eastry, 8
College Grove, 5, 8
College Grove, 7, 8
College Grove, Firs Lodge (Rear) 3
College Grove, Firs Lodge, 3
College Road, 12, 5
College Road, 2, Mythe Court 6
College Road, 20, 8
College Road, 28, Ashfield Mews, 5
College Road, 28, Ashfield, 5.6
College Road, No8 Boarding Hse, 5
College Road new Boarding House 12.6
College Road, Radnor Lodge, 6
College Road, Roslin House, 5
College Road, Royds Lodge, 6
College Road, The Nook, 6
College Road, Townsend House, 5
Como Road, 30, Viewfield, 5+6
Como Road, Como House, 6
Como Road, The White House, 5
Court Road , Outbuildings, 5
Court Road, 54 And 56, 5
Court Road, 6, Downes Cottage, 3
Court Road, 61 And 63, (Rear) 5

Court Road, 61 And 63, 7
Court Road, 8, The Barn, 5
Court Road, 90/92, The Gables, 8.6
Court Road, Court Farm Wall, 3
Court Road, Fountain Inn, 9.6
Court Road, The Barn, 3
Cowleigh Road, 54, 5.6
Edith Walk, Small Theatre, 9
Edith Walk, Waitrose Store 11.14
Graham Road, 114, Pembridge hotel, 5
Graham Road, 116, Seaforth house, 5
Graham Road,11.10
Graham Road, 142, 6
Graham Road, 17, 3
Graham Road, 29, Belford House,5
Graham Road, 45, Cedar Lodge, 5
Graham Road, 69, Beacons field, 5
Graham Road, 71, Granta Lodge, 6
Graham Road, 76, 9.6
Graham Road, 78, 9.6
Graham road, 83, Fairlea, 5
Graham Road, Cotford Hotel, 6.12
Graham Road, Edith Lodge, 3
Graham Road, Great Malvern Hotel, 5
Graham Road, The Exchange 9.6
Grange Road, Coachhouse Theatre, 5
Grange Road, Priors Croft, 6.12
Grange Road, Malvern Theatres 11.14
Great Malvern Cemetery, 5
Great Malvern Station, The Worm, 5
Hornyold Avenue, 18 and 20, 7.5
Hornyold Avenue, 22 and 24, 7
Hornyold Avenue, 27, 8
Hornyold Avenue, 6 – 12, 5
Hornyold road, 26 railings, 7
Hornyold road, 40,9.6
Hornyold Road, 41, 8
Hornyold road, 49, 5
Hornyold road, 59, 6
Hospital bank, 6 and 8, 5
Imperial Road, Fairhaven, 7.5
Imperial Road, Hatfield House, 11.10
Imperial Road, St Margaret's, 7.5
Jubilee Drive, Wyche Free Church,8.6
Laburnum Walk, 61 – 63, 9
Lansdowne Cres, Old Com Hospital 9.6
Lansdowne Crescent, Meth Church, 5

Lansdowne Crescent, Terraces, 5.6
Longridge Road, 132, 8
Longridge Road, 83, 5
Lower Wilton Road, 14, 7
Manby Road, 14 – 22, 7.5
Manby Road, 2, 1.14, 18
Manby Road, 8, 6.12
Manby Road, Malvern Parish Sch, 6.12
Manby Road, Railings, 9.6
Moorlands Road, Gardiners Cotts 8.6
Moorlands Road, Ivy House, 2
Moorlands Road, Link Villa Coachhse, 2
Moorlands Road, the clock tower, 7
Newtown road, 143 – 53, 9
Newtown road, 163, 10.6
Newtown road, 6 – 10, 5
Newtown road, 79 and 79 a, 5
Newtown road, Cox of Malvern, 5
North Malvern Road, 72 – 74, 5
North Malvern Road, But Shelter, 9
North Malvern Road, Dixie Court, 7.5
North Malvern Road, Schoolhouse, 7
Orchard Road, Bowling Club Pav 10.6
Orchard Road, 10, Orchard Grange, 4.5
Orchard Road, Friends Meeting Hse, 10.6
Orchard Road,12.4
Orchard Road, Huntington, 5
Oxford Road, 14, 16, 18, 1.3, 14-5
Peach Field Road,26 8.6
PeachField Road, Greyroofs 8.6
Peach Field Road, 71, 10.6
Peach Field Road, 81, 8
Piers Close, 4, 10
Piers Close, 7, 10
Priory Graveyard, Brick Chimney, 5
Priory Road, (Next To Splash),8
Priory Road, (Next To Splash), 8
Priory Road, The Splash,11.14
Priory Road, 15, 7
Priory Road, 19 And 17, 7
Priory Road, 26, 8.6
Priory Road, 27, Daresbury, 6
Priory Road Estate.12.6
Priory Road, 32, Portswood, 6.12
Priory Road, 36, St Ronan's, 6.12
Priory Road, 40, 6
Priory Road, Lyndsay Arts Centre, 11

Pump Street, 32, 5
Regency Road Estate, 11.6
Sling Lane, Lorne Lodge, 6.12
Somers Park Road School 9.6
Somers Park Rd, Methodist Church, 10.5
Somers Road, 15 and 17, 8.6
Somers Road, 19, 8
Somers Road, 20, 5
Somers Road, 21, Haven Hurst, 8
Somers Road, 3, 8
Somers Road, 8, The Skilts, 9
Somers Road, Link Tower, 5.6
Stanley Road, 10.6
St Andrews Road, 25 And 27, 9.6
St Andrews Road, 27, Railings, 9.6
St Andrews Road, 53/55/57,   5
St Andrews Road, 60, 10.6
St Andrews Road, 61 – 63, 7
St Andrews Road,64, 10.6
St Andrews Road, 95, 8
St Andrews Road, 95, Motorhome, 9
St Andrews Road, Old Sanatorium, 7
St Andrews Road, The Rosary, 10
St Anns Road, 23, 8
St Anns Road, 32, St Werstans, 8
St Anns Road, 34, Happy Valley Cott, 8
St Anns Road, Electrical Box, 9
St James's Road, 3, 7, 9, 11, 32, 34, -5
St Peter's Road, 19, Whitfield, 8
St Peter's Road, 3, 8.6
St Peter's Road, 5 Rothbury, 8
St Peter's Road, St Peter's house, 8.6
Thirlestane Rd, Preston Block, 10.6
Thirlestane Road, Rogers Theatre, 9.6
Tibberton Road, 10, 5.6
Tibberton Road, 2, 8.6
Tibberton Road, Tibberton House, 16, 7.5
Townsend Way, Retail Park,11.14
Townsend Way Malvern Spa 12.6
Trinity Road, Trinity Hall, 8.6
Victoria Road, 10, 5
Victoria Road, 16, 11.6
Victoria Road, 20, 11
Victoria Road, 3, Grassendale, 5
Victoria Road, Good Rest, 6
Victoria Road, Police Station, 11.6
Victoria Road,Cartwright Court 12.6

Victoria Road, Rock Burn,6.12
Wells Road, 57, 4.5
Wells Road,29 Melton Lodge, 3.6
Wells Road, The Firs, 3.6
Wilton Road, 1, Wilton Place, 8.6
Wilton Road, 12 And 14, 7
Wilton Road, 16 And 18, 7
Wilton Road, 20, 7
Wilton Road, 20, Coachhouse, 7
Wilton Road, 22, 7
Wilton Road, Cemetery Gates, 6
Wilton Road, Cemetery Lodge, 6
Wilton Road, Cemetery Noticeboard, 6
Woodshears Rd, Engineer Wrkshop, 9
Woodshears Road, 36, 8
Woodshears Road, 40, 8
Woodshears Road, Boarding House 5, 7
Woodshears Road, Orwell Lodge, 5.6
Woodshears Road, Sports Hall 12.6
Woodshears Road, The Chantry, 6
Worcester Road, 107, 5
Worcester Road, Bakery Inn,9.6
Worcester Road,Isabelle Harrison 11.6
Worcester Road, Clarendon Village 12.6
Worcester Road, Fire Station,12.6
Worcester Road,Community Hosp,12.6
**Worcester Road, Malvern Link Station
12.6**
Worcester Road, 125, The Hollies, 6,12
Worcester Road, 141, Summerfield, 6
Worcester Road, 145 – 147, 8.6
Worcester Road, 16 – 22, 10.6
Worcester Road, 167, 3
Worcester Road, 169, St Just, 5.6
Worcester Road, 171, Inchbrook, 5
Worcester Road, 76, 3
Worcester Road, Bellevue Bus Shelter, 7
Worcester Road, Brays Store, 5.6
Worcester Road, Promenade, 7.5
Worcester Road, The Chase 12.6
Worcester Road, The Lodge, 5
Worcester Road, Trafalgar House, 3
Zetland Road.11.10
Zetland Road, 2, 6

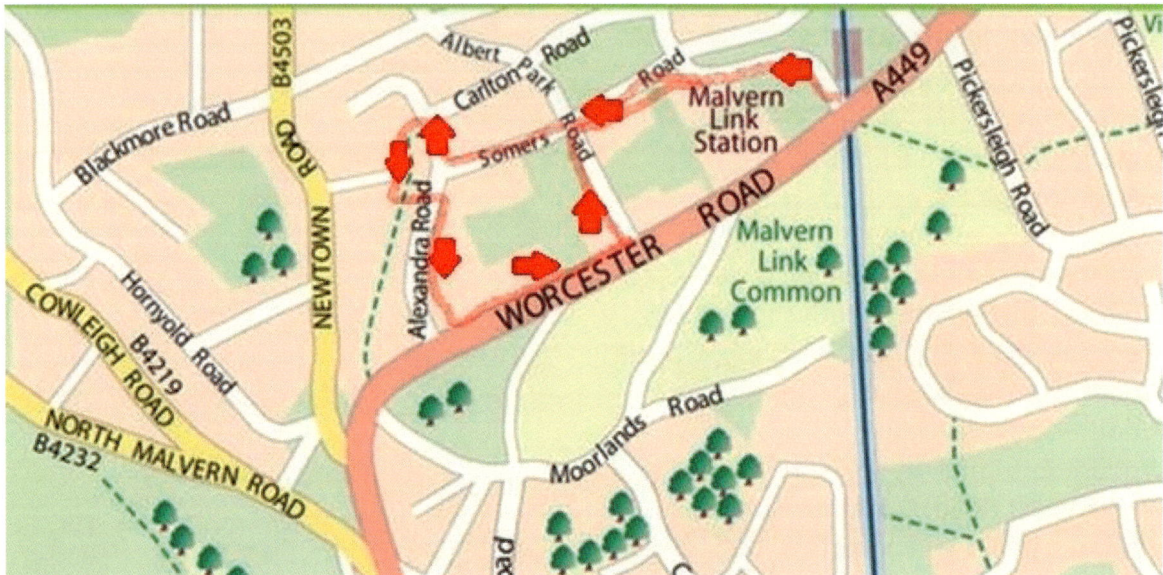

Fig 84 Map 1 OS 377500-247500 with Directions from Malvern Link Station
Somers Road, Albert Park Road, Worcester Road

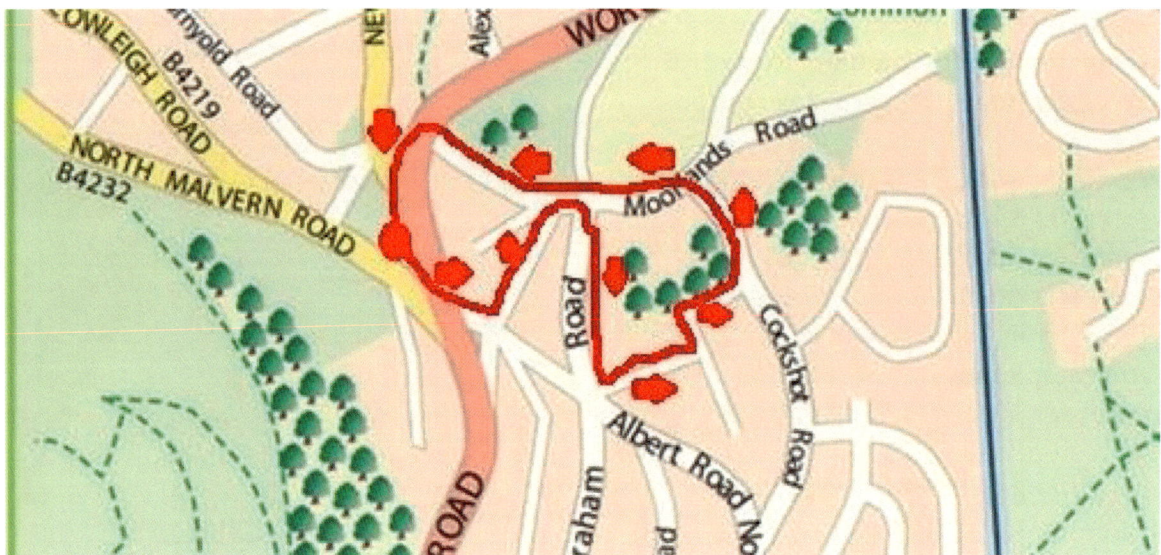

Fig 85 Map 2 377000-246500 with directions from Holy Trinity Church Link Top
Link top, Bank Street, Graham Road, St James Road, Moorlands Road

Fig 86 Map3 377500-246000 so7746sea5 with directions from Car park Victoria Road Como Road ,Graham Road, Victoria Road

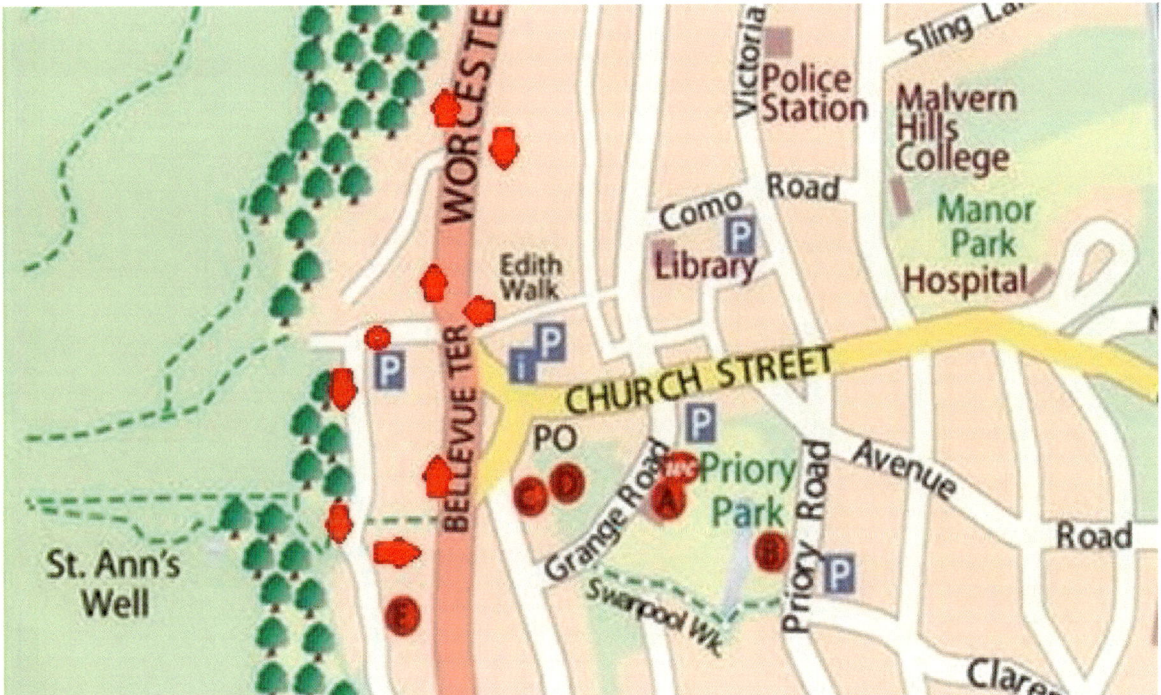

Fig 87 map 4 377000-246000 Directions from BelleVue Terrace Car park St Anns Road,99 Steps, Bellevue Terrace, Worcester Road

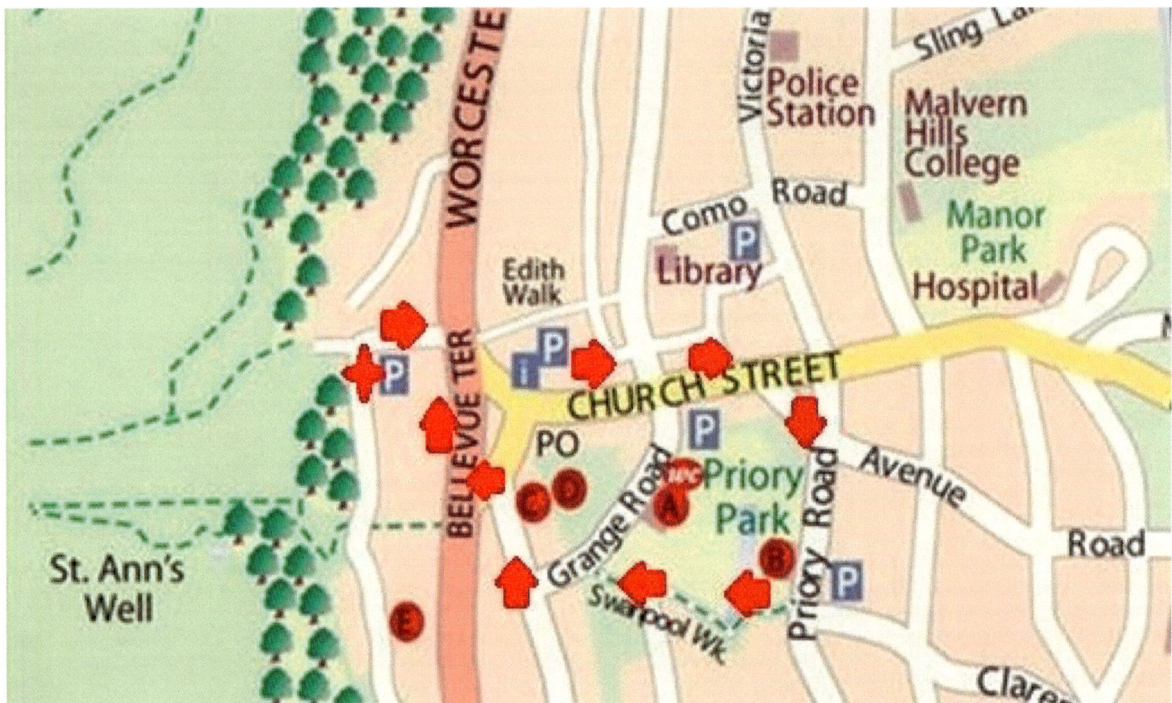

Fig 88 map 5 377500-245500 with directions from Unicorn Inn Car park Central Malvern, Church Street, Priory Road, Priory Park, Grange Road, Bellevue Terrace

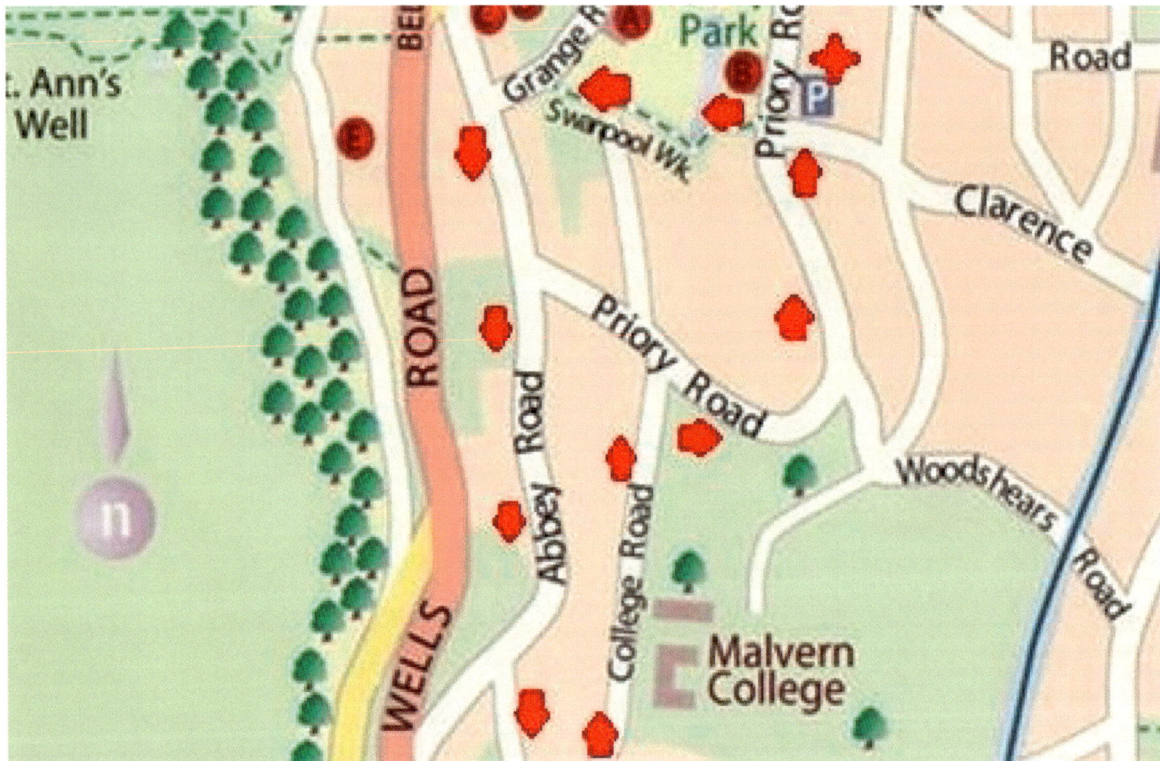

Fig 89 Map 6 245000-378000 with directions from Priory Road carpark
Priory park, Abbey Road, College Road, Priory Road

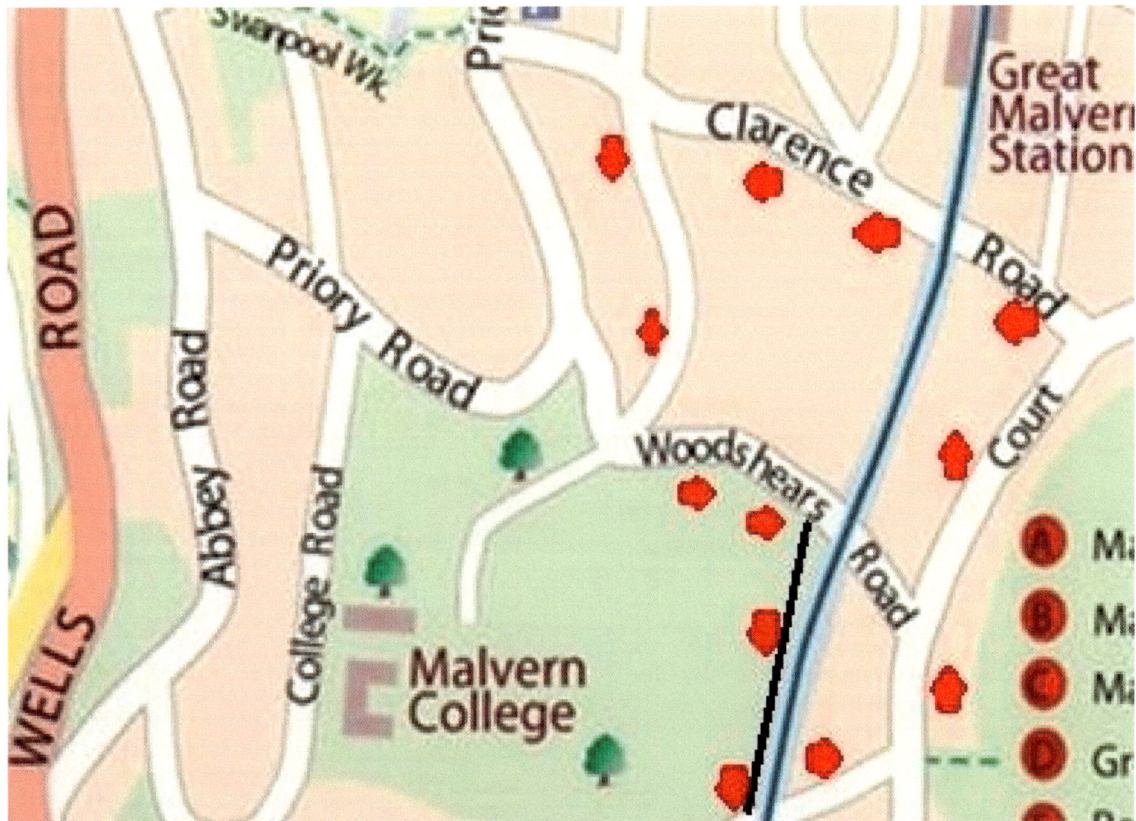

Fig 90 Map 7 378000-245500 with directions from great Malvern Station
Clarence Road, Albert Rd South, Woodshears Road, footpath to Thirlstane Road, Court Road

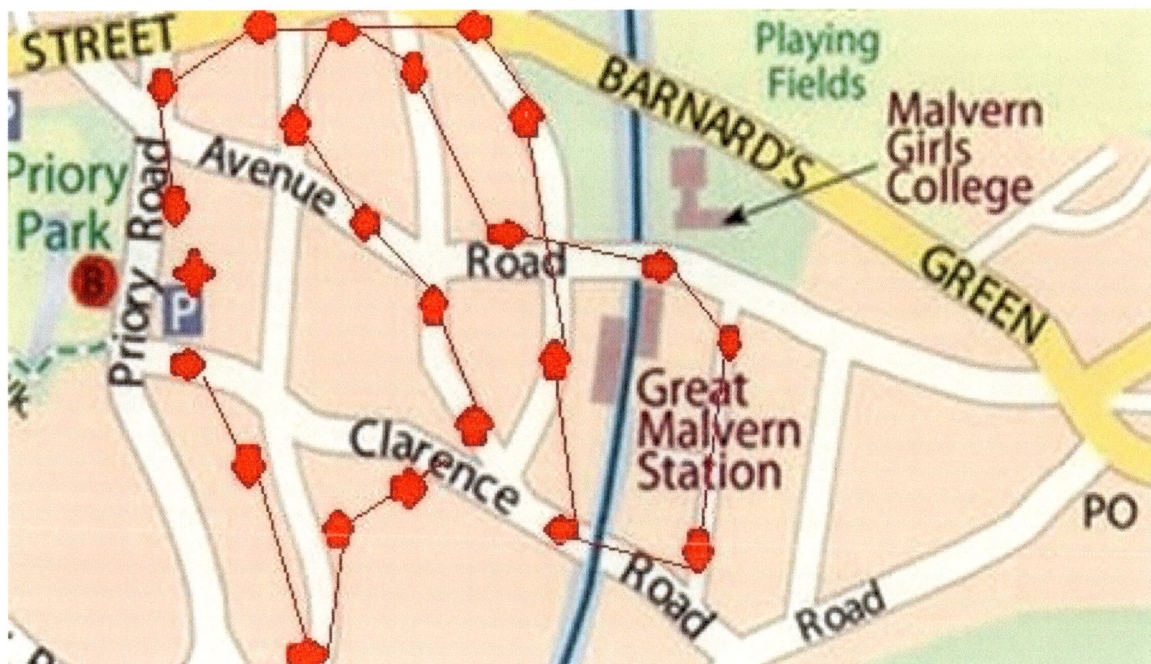

Fig 91 Map 8 378000-246000 with directions from great Malvern Station OR Priory Road carpark
Priory road, Avenue Road, Imperial Road, Christchurch Road, Clarence Road Area

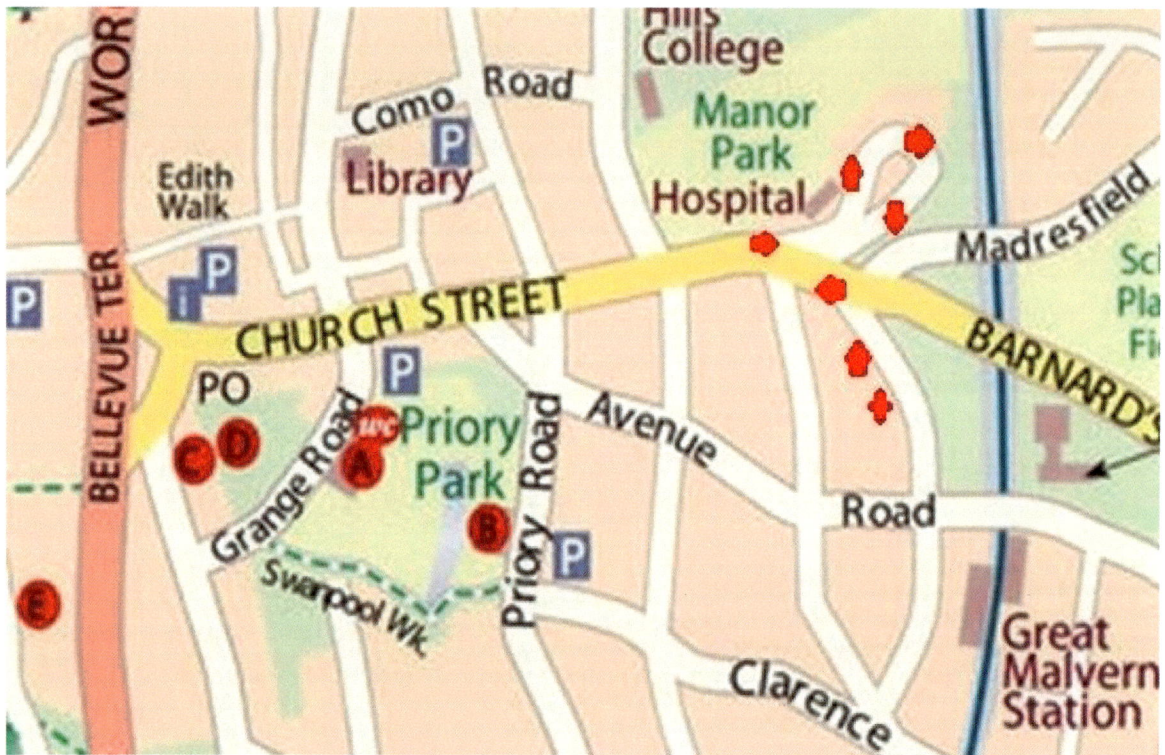

Fig 92   Map 9 246000-378500 with directions from Imperial Road. Edinburgh Dome
Lansdowne Crescent and The Old Community Hospital.

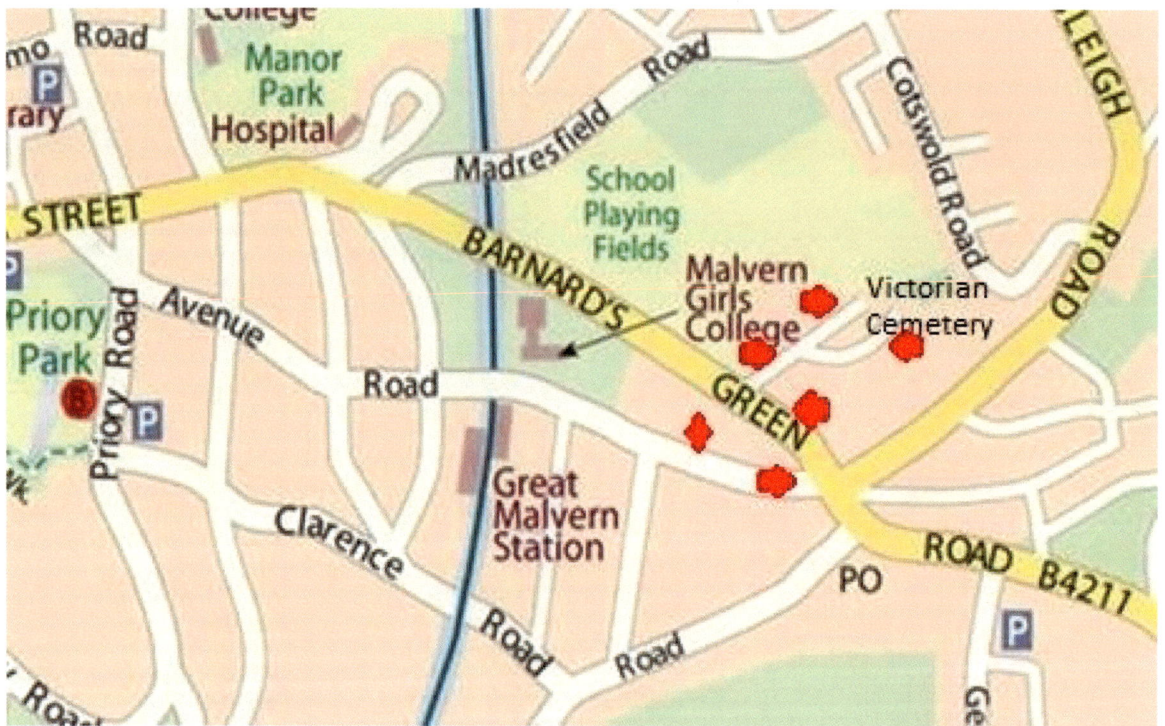

Fig 93 Map 10 378500-245500 with Directions from Avenue Road, ChristChurch
Barnards Green Rd, Wilton Road and Victorian Cemetery

Bibliography

Primary Sources

Emma Hancox, 2013. *The Historic Buildings of Worcestershire,* s.l.: Historic Environment and Archaeology Services Worcester.

Minnis,J. 23rd June 2014*Email to author about Malvern Motor Houses,s.l:s.n.*

Secondary Sources

Avery, D., 2003. Victorian & Edwardian Architecture. In: s.l.:Chancer Press.

Betjeman, J., 1972. *A Pictorial History of – English Architecture.* s.l.:Penguin books.

Brunskill, R., 1981. Traditional Buildings of Britain. In: s.l.:Victor Gollanz.

Brunskill, R., n.d. Timber Building in Britain. In: s.l.:s.n.

Brunskill,R 1970. Illustrated Handbook of Vernacular Architecture. In: s.l.:Faber.

C20th Century Society, 2012. The Seventies. In: *The Seventies.* s.l.:C20th Century Society.

C20th Century Society, 2013. Oxford and Cambridge. In: *Oxford and Cambridge.* s.l.:C20th Century Society.

Clarke, J., 2014. Early Structural Steel in London Buildings. In: s.l.:English Heritage.

Clark, K., 1950. The Gothic Revival. In: London: Constable and Company Ltd.

Cole, E., 2003. *A Consise History Of Architectural Styles.* London: A&C Black.

Conservation Bulletin, 2014. housing. *Conservation Bulletin*, summer.

Dixon, J., 2011. *The Churches and Chapels of Malvern.* s.l.:s.n.

Downes, K., 1985. *The Architectural Outsiders.* London: Waterstones.

Fellows, R., 1995. *Edwardian Architecture Style and Technology.* s.l.:Lund Humphries publishers committed.

Griffith, T., 1940. *The Priory Gateway Great Malvern,* Malvern: Troyte Griffith.

Hardie, J. M., 2012. Troyte Griffths Malvern Architect and Elgar's Friend. In: s.l.:Aspect Design Malvern.

Harris, R., 1978. Discovering Timber -Framed Buildings. In: s.l.:Shire Publication ltd.

Hoskins, L., 1998. *Living Rooms 20th Century Interiors at the Geffrye Museum.* s.l.:Geffrye Museum Trust Ltd.

Hradsky, Robert 2010. The Stamp Of Official Architecture: English Post Offices. In: *living, leisure and law eight building types in England 1800 – 1914.* s.l.:Spire books Ltd/Victorian Society.

Hurle, P., 1985. Portrait of Malvern. In: London: Phillimore & Co Ltd.

J.B.Oddfish, 1863. *Malvern Punch.* London: Simpkin,Marshall & Co.

John Brandon-Jones, 1978. *C.F.A.Voysey: Architect and Designer 1857-1941.* s.l.:Lund Humphries Ltd.

Johnson, A., 2006. *Understanding the Edwardian and Inter-war house.* s.l.:The Crowood Press ltd.

Lawrence, R. R., 2009. *The Book Of The Edwardian And Interwar House.* London: Aurum press Ltd.

Laws, A., 2003. Understanding Small Period Houses. In: s.l.:The Crowood Press Ltd.

Loudon, J., 1833. *Architectural Encyclopaedia of Cottage, Farm and Villa Architecture.* London: s.n.

McCarthy, M., 1987. *The Origins of The Gothic Revival.* london: Yale University Press.

Miller, M., 1992/2006. *Hampstead Garden Suburb Arts And Crafts Utopia?.* West Sussex: Cambridge University press.

Moody, C., 1953. *The Silouette of Malvern.* Malvern: The Priory Press Malvern.

Nott, J., 1885. *Some Of The Antiquities of Moche Malverne.* 1st ed. Malvern: Woods and Co.

Nott, J., 1900. *The Story of the Water Cure.* Malvern: Stevens & Co.

Pawley, Martin 1992. The Electronic Cottage. In: *The Name of the Room.* s.l.:BBC Book

Parissien, S., 1992. *Regency Style.* 3rd ed. London: Phaidon.

Pevsner, Alan Brooks and Nicolas, 2007. *The Buildings of England: Worcestershire.* s.l.:Yale University press.

Pevsner, N., 1951-74. *Buildings of England.* s.l.:s.n..

Rt Hon The Earl Beauchamp, 1953. Preface. In: *The Silouette of Malvern.* s.l.:The Priory Press.

Smith, B., 1964. *A History of Malvern.* Worcester: Leicester University Press.

Southall, M., 1825. *A Description of Malvern.* s.l.:G. Nicholson Stourport .

Stanley, J., 1852. *Stanleys Worcester and Malvern Guide.* 1st ed. London: John Stanley.

Stephen Calloway Mitchell Beazley, 1996. *The Elements Of Style Encyclopaedia Of Domestic Architectural Detail.* s.l.:octopus publishing group Ltd.

Teulon, A., 2009. *The Life and Work of Samuel Sanders Teulon, Victorian Architect.* Northampton: Design to Print Ltd.

The Victorian Society, 2010. *Living, Leisure and law Eight Building Types in England 1800-1914.* s.l.:Spire Books Ltd.

Tinniswood, A., 1999. *The Arts And Crafts House.* London: Octopus publishing group Ltd.

Watkin, D., 1979 revised 2001. *English Architecture A Concise History.* London: Thames and Hudson Ltd.

WindsorHarcup, J., 2010. *The Malvern Water Cure.* second ed. Great Malvern: Capella archive

Yorke, T., 2006. The 1930s House Explained. In: s.l.:Countryside Books.

Yorke, T., 2008. *British Architectural Styles.* 2nd ed. Newbury: countryside books.

Yorke, T., 2010. *The 1940s & 1950s House explained.* s.l.:Countryside Books.

Yorke, T., 2011. *Arts and crafts house styles.* s.l.:Countryside books.

Websites

http://hayslanfields.weebly.com/, 2014. *http://hayslanfields.weebly.com/.* [Online] [Accessed 12th August 2014].

http://hurstpm.net/36-supermarkets, n.d. *http://hurstpm.net/36-supermarkets.* [Online] [Accessed 25 July 2014].

http://www.bbc.co.uk/history/ww2peopleswar/stories/13/a7604813.shtml, 2005. *http://www.bbc.co.uk/history/ww2peopleswar/stories/13/a7604813.shtml.* [Online] [Accessed 23 July 2014].

http://www.british-history.ac.uk/report.aspx?compid=42867#n101, 1924. *http://www.british-history.ac.uk/report.aspx?compid=42867#n101.* [Online] [Accessed 7th August 2014].

http://www.british-history.ac.uk/report.aspx?compid=42867#n28, 2014. *http://www.british-history.ac.uk/report.aspx?compid=42867#n28.* [Online] [Accessed 28 July 2014].

http://www.british-history.ac.uk/report.aspx?compid=49879#n7, 1973. *http://www.british-history.ac.uk/report.aspx?compid=49879#n7.* [Online] [Accessed 4th August 2014].

Lennie, L., n.d. *www.buildingconservation.com/shopfronts.* [Online]
[Accessed 15th June 2013].

http://www.malverngazette.co.uk/news/9802451.Housing_plans_will_be_taken_forward/, 2012.
http://www.malverngazette.co.uk/news/9802451.Housing_plans_will_be_taken_forward/.
[Online]
[Accessed 12 August 2014].

http://www.malvern-theatres.co.uk/, 2014. *http://www.malvern-theatres.co.uk/.* [Online]
[Accessed 23 July 2014].

http://www.thegrovemalvern.co.uk/The_Grove_Malvern/History.html, n.d.
http://www.thegrovemalvern.co.uk/The_Grove_Malvern/History.html. [Online]
[Accessed 5th May 2013].

http://www.victoriansociety.org.uk/pdf/architects.pdf, n.d.
http://www.victoriansociety.org.uk/pdf/architects.pdf. [Online]
[Accessed 6th August 2014].

.